EVERYTHING YOU
CONF...

A Guide for Youth and Parents

A Living Sacraments Book by
Bart Tesoriero

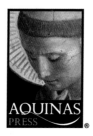

AQUINAS
PRESS ®

ISBN 978-1-61796-300-1
© 2019 Aquinas Press
Printed in China

EVERYTHING YOU NEED TO KNOW ABOUT CONFIRMATION

FOR THE CANDIDATES

FOR PARENTS

"You will receive power when the holy Spirit comes upon you, and you will be my witnesses in Jerusalem, throughout Judea and Samaria, and to the ends of the earth."

—Acts 1:8

DEAR CANDIDATE FOR THE SACRAMENT OF CONFIRMATION,

Welcome! Your faith life, your story as a Christian began at your Baptism, when the Church welcomed you into the family of God. Now you have the opportunity to receive Jesus yourself, to assent to what was given to you, a new life of grace. God respects your freedom and would never force Himself on you.

God is a Giver! He likes to give gifts. Think about it: He has given you the gift of life. He has given you natural gifts: your health, your mental and physical abilities—even your good looks! Through Baptism, God has given you the gift of faith, His divine life in your soul. He has given you your family, friends, home, possessions— the list goes on and on.

In Confirmation, you are responding to the Heavenly Father, who has used your parents, your family, the Church, and others, to bring His presence to you. One of God's greatest gifts is the gift of His Holy Spirit, because it is the gift of Himself. The Holy Spirit is God's love, in fact, the very love that God the Father and the Son share with each other. Isn't that amazing?

God poured out the Holy Spirit on Mary and the apostles at the first Pentecost—the birthday of the Church! Today this grace of Pentecost is passed on to you in the Sacrament of Confirmation, to help you enjoy the fullness of God's life and witness to your faith in Jesus Christ.

We offer this book to help you prepare for and live out this gift of the Holy Spirit. It includes a brief Overview of Confirmation, Daily Prayers, the Rite of Confirmation, Preparation for Confession and Communion, a Q and A on Confirmation, and Prayers to the Holy Spirit. This book contains the Rosary, the Stations of the Cross, Scriptural readings, and a review of Catholic teaching—all to help you receive and grow in the Holy Spirit.

May God bless you as you begin to live as a fully initiated Catholic Christian. May He help you develop all your natural and supernatural gifts and talents to enjoy fully the life He has for you and to bring His life to others. Amen!

A WORD ON PRAYER

Prayer is a communication between two people in a relationship. If you were baptized as a child and raised in a Catholic home, you probably learned how to pray at an early age. As you prayed, you began to connect in a verbal way with the God who had loved you before you were born and who brought you forth into the world through your mother and father. He has a plan for you! He wants a relationship with you. He wants you to come to know Him.

Prayer is similar to learning how to drive, which is simple: (1) Turn ignition key. (2) Step on gas pedal.

Okay, driving isn't that simple. But is prayer? Prepare for that great all-purpose answer: "Yes and no." Yes, it's simple: you talk to God. And no because…well, because of more factors than will fit on this page.

The Church grew out of the sacrifice of Jesus on the cross and a fiery encounter with the Holy Spirit on the first Pentecost. In the ensuing years and centuries, the body of believers wrote down prayers, some from Scriptures, and some from their hearts, which we pray now as the Body of Christ.

What is the best, single, individual prayer that a single, individual person can say? Here it is: The one you completely, totally mean. It doesn't matter if someone else wrote the prayer, or if you're making it up as you go along. The important thing is to pray from your heart. And to do that, you need to start with the basics.

DAILY PRAYERS

The Sign of the Cross

In the name of the Father, and of the Son ✝, and of the Holy Spirit, Amen.

The Lord's Prayer

Our Father, who art in heaven, hallowed be Thy Name;
Thy Kingdom come;
Thy Will be done on earth as it is in heaven.
Give us this day our daily bread; and forgive us our trespasses, as we forgive those who trespass against us;
and lead us not into temptation, but deliver us from evil.
For the kingdom, the power, and the glory are Yours, now and forever. Amen.

The Hail Mary

Hail Mary, full of grace, the Lord is with thee.
Blessed art thou among women, and blessed is the fruit of thy womb, Jesus.
Holy Mary, Mother of God, pray for us sinners,
now and at the hour of our death. Amen.

Glory Be to the Father

Glory be to the Father, and to the Son, and to the Holy Spirit; as it was in the beginning, is now, and ever shall be, world without end. Amen.

An Act of Faith

O my God, I firmly believe that You are one God in three Divine Persons, Father, Son, and Holy Spirit. I believe in Jesus Christ Your Son, who became man and died for our sins, and who will come to judge the living and the dead. I believe these and all the truths which the Holy Catholic Church teaches, because You have revealed them, who can neither deceive nor be deceived. Amen.

An Act of Hope

O my God, trusting in Your infinite goodness and promises, I hope to obtain pardon of my sins, the help of Your grace, and life everlasting, through the merits of Jesus Christ, my Lord and Redeemer. Amen.

An Act of Love

O my God, I love You above all things, with my whole heart and soul, because You are all-good and worthy of all my love. I love my neighbor as myself for love of You. I forgive all who have injured me, and I ask pardon of all whom I have injured. Amen.

Morning Offering to the Sacred Heart

O Jesus, through the Immaculate Heart of Mary, I offer You my prayers, works, joys, and sufferings of this day: for all the intentions of Your Sacred Heart, in union with the Holy Sacrifice of the Mass throughout the world, in reparation for my sins, for the intentions of all our associates, and in particular for the intentions of our Holy Father. Amen.

My Daily Consecration to Mary

O Mary, My Queen and my Mother, I give myself entirely to you, and to show my devotion to you I consecrate to you this day my eyes, my ears, my mouth, my heart, my whole body, without reserve. Wherefore, good Mother, as I am your own, keep me and guard me as your property and possession. Amen.

Guardian Angel Prayer

O Angel of God, my Guardian dear, to whom God's love commits me here, ever this day be at my side, to light and guard, to rule and guide. Amen.

EVENING PRAYERS

Watch, O Lord, with those who wake,
or watch, or weep tonight,
and give Your Angels and Saints charge over those who sleep.
Tend Your sick ones, O Lord Christ.
Rest Your weary ones,
Bless Your dying ones,
Soothe Your suffering ones,
Pity Your afflicted ones,
Shield Your joyous ones,
And all for Your love's sake.
Amen.
—Saint Augustine

O God, come to my assistance;
O Lord make haste to help me.
Glory be to the Father, and to the Son,
and to the Holy Spirit;
as it was in the beginning,
is now and ever shall be,
world without end.
Amen.

Take a moment to review your day. Thank God for the good things that have happened, and ask His forgiveness for any times you have failed to love Him or others.

Dear God, thank You for keeping me safe today and for giving me so many blessings and graces. Please forgive all my sins and fill me with Your love. Give me and those I love a restful sleep. Through the intercession of Our Blessed Mother Mary, have mercy on us that we may arise with renewed faith, hope, and love. Amen.

Prayer to Saint Michael the Archangel

Saint Michael the Archangel, defend us in battle. Be our safeguard against the wickedness and snares of the devil. May God rebuke him, we humbly pray; and do you, O Prince of the heavenly host, by the power of God cast into hell Satan and all the evil spirits who wander through the world seeking the ruin of souls. Amen.

The Beatitudes

When Jesus saw the crowds, he went up the mountain, and after he had sat down, his disciples came to him. He began to teach them, saying:

"Blessed are the poor in spirit,
for theirs is the kingdom of heaven.
Blessed are they who mourn,
for they will be comforted.
Blessed are the meek,
for they will inherit the land.
Blessed are they who hunger and thirst for righteousness,
for they will be satisfied.
Blessed are the merciful,
for they will be shown mercy.
Blessed are the clean of heart,
for they will see God.
Blessed are the peacemakers,
for they will be called children of God.
Blessed are they who are persecuted for the sake of righteousness,
for theirs is the kingdom of heaven.
Blessed are you when they insult you and persecute you and utter every kind of evil against you (falsely) because of me. Rejoice and be glad, for your reward will be great in heaven. Thus they persecuted the prophets who were before you."

–Matthew 5:1-13

CONFIRMATION IN SCRIPTURE AND SACRAMENT

Confirmation perfects Baptismal grace; it is the Sacrament which gives the Holy Spirit in order to root us more deeply in the divine filiation, incorporate us more firmly into Christ, strengthen our bond with the Church, associate us more closely with her mission, and help us bear witness to the Christian faith in words accompanied by deeds. (Catechism of the Catholic Church [CCC] #1316)

Confirmation...

Unites us more firmly to Christ Jesus.

Increases the gifts of the Holy Spirit.

Bonds us more perfectly with the Church.

Strengthens us to spread and defend the faith.

You are a unique gift! You are created to serve.

THE GIFT OF THE HOLY SPIRIT

Baptism, Confirmation, and Eucharist are the Sacraments of Initiation—they establish our foundation in Christ. We are born anew, or regenerated, in Baptism, strengthened in Confirmation, and nourished with the Holy Eucharist.

Through disobedience, our first parents, Adam and Eve, lost God's grace (but never His love). Through the Sacraments of Initiation, won through the obedience of Christ, God restores His grace in our souls. We are alive again!

Baptism, Confirmation, and Eucharist are not an end, but rather, a beginning: an invitation to a life of conversion, transformation, and the most exciting adventure possible: to become fully human and fully holy. Confirmation gives us the fullness of the Holy Spirit.

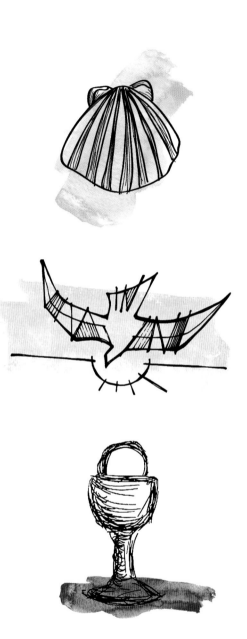

THE HOLY SPIRIT IN SCRIPTURE

The book of Genesis speaks of the Holy Spirit in the very first chapter of the Bible:

The earth was a formless wasteland, and darkness covered the abyss, while a mighty wind swept over the waters.
–Genesis 1:2

The "mighty wind" refers to the Holy Spirit, the love of God the Father and the Son for each other, and the love proceeding from them both. The Holy Spirit is the Third Person of this Blessed Trinity, a Person mighty, but also gentle. In the Old Testament, the Spirit spoke through the prophets, who testified that the Spirit would rest

upon the Messiah and His messianic people.

Referring to the Messiah—the anointed one—Isaiah the prophet proclaims:

> *The spirit of the LORD shall rest upon him:*
> *a spirit of wisdom and of understanding,*
> *A spirit of counsel and of strength,*
> *a spirit of knowledge and of fear of the LORD,*
> *and his delight shall be the fear of the LORD.*
>
> –Isaiah 11:2-3

Isaiah prophesied that the Holy Spirit would rest upon Jesus, anointing Him for His ministry of teaching, healing, and redeeming the children of God. Centuries later, God sent His Holy Spirit upon Mary, who conceived Christ—the anointed one—in her womb.

After His baptism in the Jordan and testing in the wilderness, Jesus proclaimed:

> *"The Spirit of the Lord is upon me,*
> *because he has anointed me*
> *to bring glad tidings to the poor.*
> *He has sent me to proclaim liberty to captives*
> *and recovery of sight to the blind,*
> *to let the oppressed go free,*
> *and to proclaim a year acceptable to the Lord."*
>
> –Luke 4:18-19

At Pentecost, God sent the Holy Spirit upon Mother Mary and the disciples, filling them with the power and love of Jesus Himself. The disciples went forth boldly and confidently to proclaim the mighty works of God and to bring God's love and forgiveness to all people. Three thousand people were baptized that very day!

THE HISTORY OF CONFIRMATION

The apostles and the early Church spread God's kingdom by passing on all the gifts Jesus had entrusted to them, including the wonderful gift of the Spirit received at Pentecost. They understood this gift as a completion, or confirmation, of Baptism, and they imparted it through the laying on of hands.

Now when the apostles in Jerusalem heard that Samaria had accepted the word of God, they sent them Peter and John, who went down and prayed for them, that they might receive the holy Spirit, for it had not yet fallen upon any of them; they had only been baptized in the name of the Lord Jesus. Then they laid hands on them and they received the holy Spirit.

–Acts 8:14-17

This was the beginning of the Sacrament of Confirmation. By the end of the second century, Confirmation emerged as a rite separate from Baptism. In the Latin rite, this sacrament is customarily conferred on baptized children between the age of seven and eighteen. The ordinary minister of Confirmation is the bishop, who represents the link between the confirmed and the apostles of the Church. The bishop may delegate a priest to represent him in administering the sacrament. Each Confirmation candidate should have a sponsor, preferably one of their godparents, who will help them on their lifelong journey of faith.

PREPARATION FOR CONFIRMATION

Confirmation preparation involves learning, sharing, serving, fellowship, spiritual growth and hopefully some fun along the way! The *Catechism of the Catholic Church* outlines it this way:

> "Preparation for Confirmation should aim at leading the Christian toward a more intimate union with Christ and more lively familiarity with the Holy Spirit.... To this end, catechesis (preparation) for Confirmation should strive to awaken a sense of belonging to the Church of Jesus Christ, the universal Church as well as the parish community." (CCC #1309)

By the end of this process you will hopefully:

- Develop a more personal faith with the help of the gifts of the Holy Spirit.

- Develop a deeper sense of belonging to the Catholic Church.

- Develop a more active relationship with Jesus through prayer.

- Become a more active, visible sign of Christ's love at home, school, and in your parish through the liturgical ministries, social activities, and opportunities to serve.

CHOOSING A SPONSOR

Part of your preparation for Confirmation is choosing a Confirmation sponsor. Your sponsor is someone who will help to guide, encourage, and mentor you in your faith. A sponsor must be a confirmed Catholic, at least 16 years old, and a practicing member of the Church, who is not your parent. When you are confirmed, your sponsor will place his or her hand on your right shoulder and tell the bishop your Confirmation name.

When deciding whom to choose as your sponsor, look for someone who loves Jesus, a relative or friend who is authentically trying to live their faith. Look for a prayerful man or woman who is willing to spend some time with you. A sponsor cares for you and listens to you, as you both continue your journey of faith. In a word, a sponsor is the special person chosen by you to represent your faith community.

At Baptism, the Church community shares the responsibility for the growth and protection of the graces given you. A sponsor walks with you during and *after* your Confirmation process, supporting and nurturing your faith.

Because Confirmation completes Baptism, the Church encourages you to choose one of your godparents as your sponsor. Godparents symbolize the presence of the Church and the Church's promise to support the newly baptized as they grow in Christ Jesus. From one perspective, Confirmation is about remembering, knowing, and recognizing the Father, the One who has been, is now, and will ever be in our life.

A sponsor should be a mature person of faith who is highly convinced that their faith makes a difference.

Your sponsor can assist you by:

- Being a role model of the Catholic faith in his or her daily life.

- Celebrating Mass with you and encouraging you to attend Mass.

- Supporting you spiritually as well as emotionally.

- Assisting you in discerning whether you feel called at this time to be confirmed.

- Accompanying you to informational meetings.

- Serving with you in various Service Projects.

Once you are confirmed, your sponsor's role is to continue to support you in your faith life. He or she can also offer suggestions and help you become an active member of the Church community.

Look for a sponsor who:

- Is your one of your godparents, if possible.
- Is someone whom you know well and who knows you well, someone you can talk to.
- Is honest.
- Is willing to serve others.

CHOOSING A CONFIRMATION NAME

An historic part of the Confirmation process is to choose a saint under whose name you will be confirmed. For example, if you choose Saint Francis, you will be confirmed, "Francis, be sealed with the gift of the Holy Spirit."

In the Bible, God would often give someone a new name when He had a special mission for them. For example, Abram became Abraham (The father of many nations); Jacob became Israel (God prevails); Simon became Peter (The rock). This is a great opportunity to get to know more about the saint you are choosing.

THE RITE AND EFFECTS OF CONFIRMATION

The essential rite of Confirmation includes the anointing with oil and the laying on of hands. The bishop or his representative uses a special oil called sacred *chrism*, which is oil mixed with balsam that has been consecrated by the bishop. He will lay his hand on your forehead and make the Sign of the Cross, saying, "Be sealed with the Gift of the Holy Spirit." As the bishop anoints you, God will pour out on you the gift of the Holy Spirit, like that received on the first Pentecost.

Confirmation imprints an indelible spiritual mark, or *character*, on your soul, signifying that Jesus has sealed you with His Spirit. It roots you more deeply in divine sonship and unites you more closely to Christ. This seal remains in you as a positive disposition for grace, a promise and guarantee of divine protection, and as a vocation to divine worship and to the service of the Church.

Therefore, you can only receive Confirmation once. Confirmation renews and invigorates the gifts of the Holy Spirit (such as those listed in Isaiah 11:2-3 and 1 Corinthians 12:7-11) in your soul, and gives you a special power to witness to your faith publicly.

"Do not work for food that perishes but for the food that endures for eternal life, which the Son of Man will give you. For on him the Father, God, has set his seal."
—John 6:27

Confirmation strengthens the supernatural life we receive in Baptism. It increases our sanctifying grace in every way, especially in deepening our capacity to remain spiritually alive, to abide in Christ.

Jesus instituted this sacrament so that his followers would witness to Him even to the ends of the earth. The Greek word for witness is *martyr*. Thus, as Father John Hardon writes, "Jesus sent the Holy Spirit on Pentecost to enable His disciples to be His martyrs until the end of time."

The power of the Holy Spirit we receive in Confirmation helps us to resist dangers and gives us the strength to grow more like Christ Jesus until He returns. This supernatural power = superhuman strength against the hostile forces of the world, the flesh (our fallen human nature) and the devil.

I am confident of this, that the one who began a good work in you will continue to complete it until the day of Christ Jesus. It is right that I should think this way about all of you, because I hold you in my heart, you who are all partners with me in grace, both in my imprisonment and in the defense and confirmation of the gospel.
—Philippians 1:6-7

By the end of the first century of Christianity, over one hundred dioceses were established along the shores of the Mediterranean Sea. Without exception, the Church spread because Christians were confirmed by the Holy Spirit to love others with heroic charity. They loved those who hated them. They loved those who persecuted them. Like Jesus, they even loved those who crucified them.

One of the gifts of Confirmation is the ability to spread the faith. A simple way to share the faith is to take the action of love for someone.

Confirmation calls us to not only evangelize unbelievers but to convert those who are alienated from God. Confirmation so deepens the faith of a sincerely believing Catholic that he or she is a conduit for deepening and strengthening the faith of others.

To sum up, the key to putting the gift of our Confirmation into practice is to share our faith with others.

Through Confirmation we receive our Savior's great blessing for both our minds and wills. Our minds become more convinced that what we believe is really true. And our wills become more courageous in protecting this truth, even with our lives.

The martyrs were bound, imprisoned, scourged, burnt, rent, butchered—and they multiplied. The Lord has willed that we should rejoice even over persecutions because, when persecutions occur, then the faith is crowned.

MIGHTY MOTTOS OF OUR FAITH:

- The ashes of martyrs drive away demons.
- The blood of martyrs is the seed of Christians.
- The death of the martyrs blossoms in the faith of the living.
- Heaven is opened to martyrs.
- All times are the age of martyrs.

Faith is preached first in witness
and then in words.
–Pope Francis

In the Sacrament of Confirmation, Jesus fills you with the same Spirit that came upon Mary and the disciples at that first Pentecost. Jesus calls you first of all to Himself, that you would find in Him a true friend, who knows your hopes and dreams, your struggles and successes. Jesus wants you to feel His personal love for *you*—yes, you! Jesus asks you to then share His love with others. Jesus died, rose, and sent His Spirit so all people could receive His salvation, live a fully human and holy life, and enjoy eternal union with Him and all His followers in heaven. And that's Good News!

CONFIRMATION WITHIN MASS

The Sacrament of Confirmation is usually celebrated during Mass. The candidates typically sit together with their sponsors, reminiscent of Mary and the disciples, who gathered in the upper room after Jesus' ascension, praying together as they awaited the gift of the Holy Spirit.

The Presentation of the Candidates

After the gospel, the pastor or another priest, deacon, or catechist, presents the candidates for Confirmation to the bishop, who then gives a brief homily, explaining the Scripture readings and giving everyone present a deeper understanding of the gift of the Holy Spirit given in Confirmation.

After the homily, the bishop asks the candidates to stand and renew their Baptismal promises.

Bishop: Do you renounce Satan
and all his works and empty promises?

Candidates: I do.

Bishop: Do you believe in God,
the Father almighty,
Creator of heaven and earth?

Candidates: I do.

Bishop: Do you believe in Jesus Christ, his only Son, our Lord,
who was born of the Virgin Mary,
suffered death and was buried,
rose from the dead,
and is seated at the right hand of the Father?

Candidates: I do.

Bishop: Do you believe in the Holy Spirit,
the Lord, the giver of life,
who today through the Sacrament of Confirmation
is given to you in a special way
just as he was given to the Apostles on the day of Pentecost?

Candidates: I do.

Bishop: Do you believe in the holy Catholic Church,
the communion of saints,
the forgiveness of sins,
the resurrection of the body,
and life everlasting?

Candidates: I do.

The bishop gives his assent to their profession of faith by proclaiming the faith of the Church:

This is our faith. This is the faith of the Church.
We are proud to profess it in Christ Jesus our Lord.

All: Amen.

The Laying on of Hands

The laying of hands on the candidates by the bishop and the concelebrating priests expresses the biblical gesture of calling down the gift of the Holy Spirit.

The concelebrating priests stand near the bishop, who prays facing the assembly:

Dearly beloved,
Let us pray to God the almighty Father,
for these, his adopted sons and daughters,
already born again to eternal life in Baptism,
that he will graciously pour out the Holy Spirit
upon them to confirm them with his abundant gifts,
and through his anointing
conform them more fully to Christ, the Son of God.

All pray silently for a short time.

The bishop and the priests who will minister the sacrament with him lay hands upon all the candidates (by extending their hands over them). The bishop alone says:

Almighty God, Father of our Lord Jesus Christ,
who brought these your servants to new birth
by water and the Holy Spirit,
freeing them from sin:
send upon them, O Lord, the Holy Spirit, the Paraclete;
give them the spirit of wisdom and understanding,
the spirit of counsel and fortitude,
the spirit of knowledge and piety;
fill them with the spirit of the fear of the Lord.
Through Christ our Lord.

All: **Amen.**

The Anointing with Chrism

Through the anointing with sacred Chrism (aromatic oil consecrated by the bishop), the candidate receives the indelible character, the seal of the Holy Spirit, along with the grace of the Holy Spirit conforming him or her more closely to Christ.

Each candidate goes to the bishop. The sponsor who presents the candidate places his (her) right hand on the latter's shoulder and gives the candidate's name to the bishop.

The bishop dips his right thumb in the Chrism and makes the Sign of the Cross on the forehead of the one to be confirmed, as he says:

N., be sealed with the Gift of the Holy Spirit.

The newly confirmed responds:
Amen.

The bishop says:
Peace be with you.

The newly confirmed responds:
And with your spirit.

The Mass proceeds as usual.

Concluding Rite

At the end of Mass, the bishop extends his hands and sings or says:

The Lord be with you.

All: And with your spirit.

The deacon or minister gives the invitation in these or similar words:
Bow your heads and pray for God's blessing.

The Bishop, with hands extended over the newly confirmed, says:

May God the Father almighty bless you,
whom he has made his adopted sons and daughters
reborn from water and the Holy Spirit,
and may he keep you worthy of his fatherly love.

All: Amen.

Bishop:
May his Only Begotten Son,
who promised that the Spirit of truth would abide in his Church,
bless you and confirm you by his power
in the confession of the true faith.

All: Amen.

Bishop:
May the Holy Spirit,
who kindles the fire of charity in the hearts of disciples,
bless you and lead you blameless and gathered as one
into the joy of the Kingdom of God.

All: Amen.

The bishop adds immediately:

And may almighty God bless all of you, who are gathered here, the Father, ✝ and the Son, ✝ and the Holy ✝ Spirit.

All: Amen.

Prayer Over the People

Instead of the preceding blessing, the prayer over the people may be used. The deacon or minister gives the invitation in these or similar words:

Bow down for the blessing.

The Bishop, with hands extended over the newly confirmed and the people, says:

Confirm, O God,
what you have brought about in us,
and preserve in the hearts of your faithful
the gifts of the Holy Spirit:
may they never be ashamed
to confess Christ crucified before the world
and by devoted charity
may they ever fulfill his commands.
Who lives and reigns for ever and ever.

All: **Amen.**

And may the blessing of almighty God,
the Father, ✝ and the Son, ✝ and the Holy ✝ Spirit,
come down on you and remain with you for ever.

All: **Amen.**

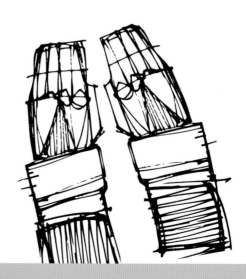

THE SACRAMENT OF RECONCILIATION

Jesus loves you! He created you to live with Him forever. He asks you to love God with all your heart, soul, mind, and strength, and to love others as yourself.

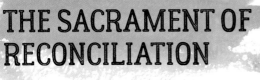

Sometimes we turn away from Jesus and fail to love as He asks us to. This sin separates us from God. But Jesus, who died for us, loves us too much to let us remain apart. He wants very much to forgive us if only we repent. This we do through the Sacrament of Reconciliation.

EXAMINATION OF CONSCIENCE

The Ten Commandments

I I am the Lord, Your God. You shall have no other gods before Me.

Do I pray every day? Do I worship God alone? Have I participated in any superstitious practices? Do I let the things of this world (entertainment, money, etc.) take precedence over love of God?

II You shall not take the name of the Lord in vain.

Do I respect God's name? Do I misuse it out of frustration or anger or to impress those around me? Am I willing to stand up for God, to speak of Him before others?

III Remember to keep holy the Lord's day.

Do I attend Mass on Sundays and Holy Days? Do I participate by praying and singing? Do I listen closely to the Scripture readings? Do I refrain from work on Sundays except when necessary, and spend time with my family and loved ones?

IV Honor your Father and Mother.

God puts people in authority to care for us, protect us, and guide us. Do I obey my parents willingly? Do I help out at home? Do I respect older people?

V You shall not kill.

Do I taunt or fight with others? Have I abused alcohol or other drugs? Do I forgive readily or do I seek revenge?

VI You shall not commit adultery.

When two people get married, they promise their mutual love to one other. God wants them to honor that promise, and wants all of us to be chaste and modest in our behavior. Do I treat my body with respect? Have I kept myself pure in thought, word, and deed?

VII You shall not steal.

Am I trustworthy and faithful to my word? Do I respect other people's property? Have I stolen or damaged what belongs to another? Have I been honest in my schoolwork?

VIII You shall not lie.

Have I lied to protect myself or 'get away' with something? Have I gossiped about others or damaged their reputation in any way?

IX You shall not covet your neighbor's wife.

Marriage is a great blessing, a very special gift from God. Do I allow my parents to spend time with one another? Do I pray for my parents?

X You shall not covet your neighbor's goods.

Do I want what others have? Am I jealous of others? Am I grateful for all God has given me? Do I share with others?

Prayer Before Confession

Dear Jesus, I come before You today and admit that I have sinned against heaven and against You. I repent of my sins. I want to walk as Your child. I want to live in freedom and joy. I want to be fully alive, made whole by Your grace and forgiveness. Grant me the honesty to know my sins, the humility to confess them, and the grace to avoid them.

Dear Mother Mary, please help me make a good confession, and be filled with the peace of Christ. Amen.

HOW TO GO TO CONFESSION

Make the Sign of the Cross as you say, **"Bless me Father, for I have sinned. It has been _____ since my last Confession."**

Confess your sins.

When you have finished, say, **"I am sorry for these and all my sins."**

The priest will give you a penance, and he may offer you some spiritual direction.

Pray an Act of Contrition

O my God, I am heartily sorry for having offended You. I detest all my sins because of Your just punishments, but most of all because they offend You, my God, who are all-good and deserving of all my love. I firmly resolve, with the help of Your grace, to sin no more and to avoid the near occasions of sin. Amen.

Prayer After Confession

Dear God,
Thank You so much for forgiving me!
I feel lighter, forgiven, renewed,
and ready to go on with my life.
I want to walk in freedom from sin,
to avoid the occasions and places
that would lead me back into it.
Lord, I admit I can't do it without You,
so please, through the prayers of Mary, my Mother,
help me to continue living in peace and joy
with You and others.
In Jesus' name. Amen.

COMMUNION PRAYERS

Prayer Before Communion

Dear Jesus, I very much want to receive You in Holy Communion. I am sorry for the ways I have hurt You and others, O Lord, by not doing what is right. Please forgive me!

Most of all thank You for always loving me. By the prayers of Your dear Mother Mary, make me worthy to receive You now.

May this Communion fill me with joy and peace as You come into my heart. Amen.

My Offering

Dear Jesus, I offer myself to You this day as I prepare to receive You in Holy Communion. Please make me ready to receive You with all the love in my heart. Amen.

My Act of Praise

Dear God, I worship You today, Father, Son, and Holy Spirit! Thank you for being my Father and Lover. I praise You for who You are, Good Shepherd and King of Love. To You be praise, to You be glory, to You be thanksgiving forever and ever. Amen.

My Act of Love

Dear Jesus, You love me so much that You have given me Your Body and Blood in Holy Communion. I love You too, Jesus. Please forgive me for the times I have not loved You or others. Help me to make a home for You in my heart, that You may always be with me, and I may always be with You. Amen.

Prayer After Communion

O Jesus, You have just come to me in Holy Communion.
Your Body is living in my body.
Your Heart is beating in my heart.
You are truly present in me now.
Thank You so much for coming into my heart!
I am so glad You are here with me.
Please don't ever leave me.

I love You, Jesus.

I want to live forever with You in heaven.

Today I give myself to You.
I give You my body, my mind, my heart.
Please keep me close to Your Heart,
and bring me back to You if ever I stray from You.
Jesus, I love You. Amen.

Song of Thanksgiving

Give thanks to the LORD, who is good,
whose love endures forever.
Let the house of Israel say:
God's love endures forever.
Let those who fear the LORD say,
God's love endures forever.
You are my God, I give you thanks;
my God, I offer you praise.

—Psalm 118:1-4, 28

Help Me, Lord

Lord, I feel lost. I have looked for love in the wrong places and sought comfort where it cannot be found. Let me, instead, find my peace in You, O my Lord. Only You can fill this hole inside my heart. Give me the courage to look to You and to trust that You are enough for me. Please give me in this Holy Communion the strength to overcome the rash desires of my mind and body, and the patience to wait while Your plan for me unfolds in Your time. O Heavenly Father, I embrace You now, and receive Your embrace. Amen.

Anima Christi

Soul of Christ, sanctify me.
Body of Christ, save me.
Blood of Christ, inebriate me.
Water from the side of Christ, wash me.
Passion of Christ, strengthen me.
O good Jesus, hear me.
Within Your wounds, hide me.
Do not permit me to be parted from You.
From the evil foe protect me.
At the hour of my death call me.
And bid me come to You,
To praise You with all Your saints,
For ever and ever. Amen.

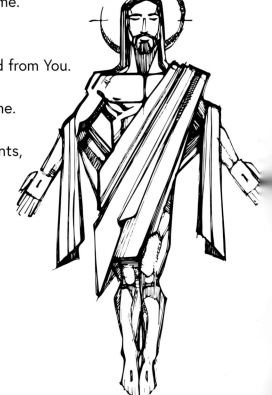

CATECHESIS Q & A ON CONFIRMATION

Catechesis comes from the Greek word *katekhein:* "to resound." Jesus promised His disciples, "You will receive *power* when the holy Spirit comes upon you" (Acts 1:8, emphasis added). Do you want that power? God wants to give it to you! When we receive Christ, we are called to be messengers of His joy. The Holy Spirit wants to empower you to resonate Christ, the Light of the world and the hope of mankind, to all. God saves us so we can save others. Saint John Paul II said that only after we are transformed through the Holy Spirit should we attempt the transformation of the world.

We want to help you be transformed. We invite you in this section to answer each question as best you can before reading the answer. See what you know! Much of this material comes from the *Compendium of the Catechism of the Catholic Church* and focuses on the gift of the Holy Spirit and the Sacrament of Confirmation.

1. Why did God create you?

God, who is love, created me because He wanted me to share in His happiness. He created me to know Him, to love Him, and to serve Him.

2. How did humanity get separated from God?

Our first parents disobeyed God and fell into sin. They became separated from God's presence within their spirits. But God did not abandon them or us. He sent His Son to redeem and save all of us, calling us into His Body, the Church, and making us His adopted children and heirs of heaven, through the work of His Holy Spirit.

3. How does God reveal Himself to you?

God reveals Himself to me through His Creation, in His Word, and most completely in His Son, Jesus Christ, the Word made flesh.

In the sending of His Son and the gift of the Spirit, "revelation is now fully complete, although the faith of the Church must gradually grasp its full significance" over the centuries. –*Compendium of the Catechism of the Catholic Church.*

It is important to note that God is a person—He is not a set of rules nor a collection of teachings. When you love someone, you share yourself with him or her, and God is no different. He wants a relationship with you, to share His divine life with you. Scripture compares God to a lover looking for his bride. He communicates Himself to humanity gradually because we just couldn't take Him all at once.

4. What is God calling you to?

God is calling me to communion with Himself.

Our dignity rests above all in this truth. God calls us to be holy—fully alive, fully human, and fully obedient to Himself. Our path to holiness goes by way of the Cross and leads to true happiness now and in eternity. Obedience is the path of blessing.

5. How can you respond to God?

Through the gift of grace, I respond to God with the obedience of faith.

Saint Augustine said, "I believe, in order to understand; and I understand, the better to believe."

6. What is faith?

Faith is a conscious, deliberate, choice to put my trust in God.

You may not always feel assured. Still, God calls us to choose to believe Him and His Word to us. It is certainly okay to tell the Lord, as did the father of an afflicted son, "I do believe, help my unbelief!" (Mark 9:24).

7. How can you know God?

I can come to know God by spending time with Him in prayer, reading and obeying His Word, receiving His sacraments, studying the Church's teachings, and reading the lives of the saints.

Jesus said, "This is eternal life, that they should know you, the only true God, and the one whom you sent, Jesus Christ" (John 17:3). Like anyone in a relationship, God wants to be known by us.

8. How can you love God?

I can grow in love for God by believing in Jesus and receiving His love. I love God by obeying His commandments and by turning from sin. I love God by caring for Him above everything else, and by loving others as I love myself.

9. How can you worship God?

I worship God by celebrating Mass and receiving Holy Communion on Sundays and, when possible, during the week, by going to Confession regularly, by praying often, and by reading His Word. I can praise and worship God alone in prayer or with others in liturgy or group prayer. I can sing His praise in formal Masses or informal worship services.

> So here's what I want you to do, God helping you: Take your everyday, ordinary life—your sleeping, eating, going-to-work, and walking-around life—and place it before God as an offering. Embracing what God does for you is the best thing you can do for him. Don't become so well-adjusted to your culture that you fit into it without even thinking. Instead, fix your attention on God. You'll be changed from the inside out. Readily recognize what he wants from you, and quickly respond to it. Unlike the culture around you, always dragging you down to its level of immaturity, God brings the best out of you, develops well-formed maturity in you.
>
> –Romans 12:1-2; MSG

10. Who is the Holy Spirit?

The Holy Spirit, the Third Person of the Blessed Trinity, is the love with which the Father and the Son love each other.

Jesus called the Holy Spirit the *Paraclete*—Consoler or Advocate— and the Spirit of Truth. The amazing thing is that the love between God the Father and God the Son is not just an energy or force field, but actually a Person!

11. What did God promise about the Holy Spirit?

Through the Prophets God promised that His Spirit would gather His scattered children into one, renew their hearts, and transform the earth. The prophets of Israel foretold that the Spirit of the Lord would rest on the Messiah, empowering him for his saving mission.

Jesus Himself proclaimed:

> *"The spirit of the Lord GOD is upon me,*
> *because the LORD has anointed me;*
> *He has sent me to bring glad tidings to the lowly,*
> *to heal the brokenhearted,*
> *To proclaim liberty to the captives*
> *and release to the prisoners."*
>
> –Isaiah 61:1

12. What is the mission of the Holy Spirit?

The Spirit is the Lord and Giver of Life. God sends His Spirit to give us new life as His beloved children.

Jesus said, "I have come to set the earth on fire, and how I wish it were already blazing!" (Luke 12:49). This fire is the Holy Spirit, given to ignite in us a passion for God and for true, life-giving love. Through the Church the Spirit prepares our hearts and manifests Christ Jesus to us, to restore all humanity to communion with God.

13. What happened at Pentecost?

On Pentecost, God poured out His Holy Spirit on Mary and the apostles. Filled with His power, they joyfully and courageously went forth to share the Good News, inviting everyone into God's communion of love.

14. What does the Holy Spirit do in the Church?

The Spirit builds up, animates, and sanctifies the Body of Christ. The Spirit forgives our sins, restores our divine likeness, and helps us love as God loves us. As the Spirit of Love, He restores God's likeness in each of us—we 'belong' now, through the Spirit!

15. How do Christ and His Spirit act in our hearts?

Christ Jesus shares His Spirit and grace with us through the sacraments. The gifts of the Spirit produce the fruits of the Spirit within us and make us holy. Saint Paul wrote, "And do not get drunk on wine, in which lies debauchery, but be filled with the Spirit" (Ephesians 5:18).

16. How do we initially receive the Holy Spirit?

We first receive the Holy Spirit in the Sacrament of Baptism, which cleanses us of Original Sin, unites us with Christ Jesus, gives us sanctifying grace, and makes us members of His Body, the Church.

17. Why do we need to receive the Spirit again at Confirmation?

In Baptism, the Holy Spirit washes away Original Sin and makes us part of the Body of Christ. In Confirmation, the Holy Spirit strengthens us and prepares us for battle against the forces of evil.

18. What are some symbols of the Holy Spirit?

The Spirit is the *Paraclete,* the Advocate who guides us into all truth. Some of His symbols are:

Wind

Fire

Oil

Light

The Dove

The Cloud

Water

19. What is grace?

Grace is God's free gift of His supernatural life and favor, which He gives to us so that we might respond to His invitation to share in His life and love and achieve eternal salvation—eternal union with Him in heaven. God's free gift of grace calls for our free response.

20. What are the different types of grace?

Sanctifying, or habitual, grace, makes us holy over time. It is a sharing in the life and love of God that is constantly available in our hearts. God also gives *actual* grace for specific circumstances, *sacramental* graces proper to each sacrament, and special graces or *charisms* intended for the common good of the Church.

21. What is a sacrament?

The seven sacraments are outward, or perceptible, signs of grace instituted by Christ and entrusted to the Church, to give grace. Sacraments are outer signs of inner grace.

Each sacrament is a guaranteed opportunity to receive grace. The benefits of a sacrament, however, depend upon the disposition and preparation of the one receiving it. Our disposition affects a sacrament's effectiveness. The Holy Spirit prepares us to celebrate the sacraments through a worthy faith.

22. What does a sacrament do for us?

A sacrament confers the sacramental grace it signifies. Christ Himsel is at work in His sacraments, making us children of God in Baptism, forgiving our sins in Reconciliation, feeding us with His Body and Blood in the Holy Eucharist, always healing us and uniting us more closely to Himself and His Church. The Holy Spirit heals us and transforms us as we receive the sacraments.

In fact, the Holy Spirit is transforming each of us into an image of Christ Jesus himself. Saint Paul writes, "All of us, gazing with unveile face on the glory of the Lord, are being transformed *into the same image* from glory to glory, as from the Lord who is the Spirit" (2 Corinthians 3:18, emphasis added).

23. What is the Sacrament of Confirmation?

The Holy Spirit came in power upon Mary and the disciples at Pentecost. The apostles in turn passed on the Holy Spirit to the newly baptized by the laying on of hands. Confirmation is the sacramental conferral of this gift of the Holy Spirit. Confirmation is the sacrament of spiritual strengthening. It is the power and life of God given to us, bringing our character more into conformity with God's through the power of the Holy Spirit.

24. What is the essential Rite of Confirmation?

The essential Roman Rite of Confirmation consists in the anointing with sacred chrism and the laying on of hands by the minister of Confirmation, who pronounces the words, "Be sealed with the Gift of the Holy Spirit."

25. What are the effects of Confirmation?

Confirmation is a special outpouring of the Holy Spirit, the grace of Pentecost, on the newly confirmed. This outpouring gives us an indelible character and produces a growth in the grace of our Baptism. This means we belong in a special way to Jesus; we are temples of His Holy Spirit and no longer belong to this world. Confirmation roots us more deeply as the children of God, binds us more firmly to Christ and the Church, reinvigorates the gifts of the Holy Spirit in our souls, and gives us a special strength to bear witness to our Christian faith.

26. What does "indelible character" mean?

A sacramental "character" is a special supernatural and ineffaceable mark, or seal, impressed upon the soul, by each of the sacraments of Baptism, Confirmation, and Holy Orders. Thus they may not be administered more than once to the same person.

This character is a spiritual mark, sign, or badge, that fits a person to be devoted to the work of worship. Confirmation, which confers spiritual strength, qualifies the recipient for the duty of honoring God by professing the Christian faith before its enemies.

27. What are the gifts of the Holy Spirit?

The Prophet Isaiah speaks of the Messiah, and lists the gifts of the Spirit in Isaiah 11:2-3. Thus, the gifts of the Spirit are the "permanent dispositions" of:

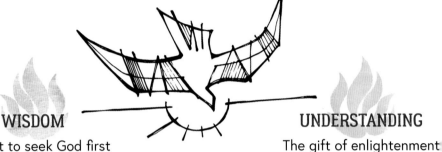

WISDOM

The gift to seek God first in all things and to see life from His perspective.

UNDERSTANDING

The gift of enlightenment to grasp God's truth.

COUNSEL

The gift of guidance to make good decisions and do what pleases God.

KNOWLEDGE

The gift to know God and know myself.

PIETY

The gift to enjoy God and the service of God.

FEAR OF THE LORD

The gift of reverence, awe, and respect towards God.

FORTITUDE

The gift of courage and strength to overcome all obstacles in following Jesus, including interior fear and exterior intimidation.

28. What is the fruit of the Holy Spirit?

Just as a tree draws in nourishment to produce fruit, so the gifts of the Spirit produce in us the fruits of:

Love • Joy • Peace

Patience • Kindness

Goodness • Generosity

Gentleness • Faithfulness

Modesty

Self-control • Chastity

(See Galatians 5:22-23.)

29. What are the Seven Sacraments?

The Seven Sacraments are Baptism, Penance, Eucharist, Confirmation, Matrimony, Holy Orders and the Anointing of the Sick.

30. What are the Theological Virtues?

The Theological Virtues are Faith, Hope and Charity.

31. What are the Cardinal Virtues?

The Cardinal Virtues are Prudence (to discern the good), Justice, Fortitude, and Temperance (moderation or self-restraint of a person's actions, thoughts or feelings).

32. What is the Nicene Creed?

I believe in one God, the Father Almighty, maker of heaven and earth, of all things visible and invisible. I believe in one Lord, Jesus Christ, the Only Begotten Son of God, born of the Father before all ages. God from God, Light from Light, true God from true God, begotten, not made, consubstantial with the Father; through Him all things were made. For us men and for our salvation He came down from heaven, and by the Holy Spirit was incarnate of the Virgin Mary, and became man. For our sake He was crucified under Pontius Pilate; He suffered death and was buried, and rose again on the third day in accordance with the Scriptures.

He ascended into heaven and is seated at the right hand of the Father. He will come again in glory to judge the living and the dead and His kingdom will have no end.

I believe in the Holy Spirit, the Lord, the giver of life, who proceeds from the Father and the Son, who with the Father and the Son is adored and glorified, who has spoken through the prophets.

I believe in one, holy, catholic and apostolic Church. I confess one Baptism for the forgiveness of sins, and I look forward to the resurrection of the dead and the life of the world to come. Amen.

33. What are the two greatest commandments?

Jesus taught that the two greatest commandments are:

> *"You shall love the Lord, your God, with all your heart, with all your soul, and with all your mind."*
>
> *"You shall love your neighbor as yourself."*
>
> –Matthew 22:37, 39

34. How can I love?

We are created to love! Saint John Paul II said that to love is **to give myself in self-donation to another.** He declared, "A person's rightful due is to be treated as an object of love, not as an object for use." The Holy Father encouraged us, "Open your minds and hearts to the beauty of all that God has made and to His special, personal love for each one of you."

35. What is prayer?

Prayer is the raising of our mind and heart to God, in **ACTS:**
* Adoration: Praise and worship.
* Contrition: Sorrow and repentance for our sins.
* Thanksgiving: Giving thanks in everything.
* Supplication: Asking for what we need.

Prayer is our personal communication with God our Father, His Son Jesus Christ, and their Holy Spirit who dwells in our hearts.

36. How does Jesus teach us to pray?

Jesus teaches us by His example and by His prayer—the *Our Father*—that God is our loving Father who only wants the best for us. Jesus teaches us to seek God daily with a pure heart, a forgiving heart, a faithful heart, and a watchful heart.

> *"Ask and you will receive, so that your joy may be complete."*
> —John 16:24

37. How does the Holy Spirit help us pray?

The Holy Spirit prays within us. Saint Paul says, "In the same way, the Spirit too comes to the aid of our weakness; for we do not know how to pray as we ought, but the Spirit itself intercedes with inexpressible groanings." (Romans 8:26)

Therefore we should always ask the Spirit to pray with us. An easy prayer is simply, "Holy Spirit, come." A simple but powerful prayer is *Come Holy Spirit,* found on page 51.

THE PRECEPTS OF THE CHURCH

God does not save us in isolation. We are part of a family, the Church. Each baptized person is a member of the Body of Christ, a living Body. In union with everyone else in the Church we discern and fulfill our calling, our vocation. We receive from the Church the Word of God, the grace of the sacraments, and the examples of holiness found in Mary and the saints. We also receive the prayer support of our brothers and sisters, companions with us on the journey of life to Life.

Our faith must affect *how we live*. Jesus said, "Not everyone who says to me, 'Lord, Lord,' will enter the kingdom of heaven, but only the one who does the will of my Father in heaven" (Matthew 7:21). Our obedience actually forms part of our worship. The Church, through the Pope and bishops, teaches us to serve God and to serve others for the good of all. The Church gives us six precepts, or rules, which specify the very minimum we need to do to love God and others.

1. You shall attend Mass on Sundays and holy days of obligation and remain free from work or activity that could impede the sanctification of such days.
2. You shall confess your sins at least once a year.
3. You shall humbly receive your Creator in Holy Communion at least during the Easter season.
4. You shall keep holy the holy days of obligation.
5. You shall observe the days of fasting and abstinence established by the Church.
6. You shall help provide for the needs of the Church.

THE SPIRITUAL AND CORPORAL WORKS OF MERCY

Since apostolic times, the Church has given us seven ways, based on Jesus' teaching, to care for both the spiritual and physical needs of our neighbor.

The Spiritual Works of Mercy

- Counsel the doubtful.
- Instruct the ignorant.
- Admonish sinners.
- Comfort the afflicted.
- Forgive offenses.
- Bear wrongs patiently.
- Pray for the living and the dead.

The Corporal Works of Mercy

- Feed the hungry.
- Give drink to the thirsty.
- Clothe the naked.
- Shelter the homeless.
- Visit the sick.
- Visit those in prison.
- Bury the dead.

PRAYERS TO THE SPIRIT OF THE LORD

Come, Holy Spirit

Come, Holy Spirit, fill the hearts of Your faithful,

and kindle in us the fire of Your love.

Send forth Your Spirit and we shall be created,

and You shall renew the face of the earth.

Let us pray. O God, who by the light of Your Holy Spirit, has instructed the hearts of Your faithful, grant us by the same Spirit to be truly wise, and ever to rejoice in His consolation, through the same Christ our Lord. Amen.

Prayer for the Gifts of the Spirit

Lord and Giver of Life, Father of the poor,
You who pour forth Your sevenfold gifts
through the Sacrament of Confirmation,
hear us as we pray:

Spirit of sonship, grant to us
Fear of the Lord that we might stand in Your presence
with wonder and awe,
and *Piety* to draw our hearts to recognize
that You are our Father and we are Your children.
Keep us in step with You by sending us
Counsel to know Your will for our lives;
Wisdom to apply that will; and
Fortitude to do Your will.

Spirit that leads us to all truth,
grant us *Knowledge* to know Your truth in our heart,
and *Understanding* to comprehend what You have revealed.

Heavenly Father, thank You for Your great love for us, and for Your plan for each of our lives. May these spiritual gifts conform us to the image of Your Son, Jesus, the firstborn among many.
In Jesus' name. Amen.

Prayer for the Fruits of the Spirit

Holy Spirit, eternal Love of the Father and the Son,
I come into Your presence. Please come upon me,
O Spirit of God, and produce in me the fruit of love,
that I may be united to You by divine love;
joy, that I may be filled with Your consolation;
peace, that I may enjoy tranquility of soul;
and patience, that I may endure everything
that may be opposed to Your desires for me.

Divine Spirit, infuse in me the fruit of kindness,
that I may willingly help others;
goodness, that I may be compassionate toward all; long-suffering,
that I may not be discouraged but may persevere in prayer;
and gentleness, that I may be even-tempered with others.

Spirit of God, graciously impart to me the fruit of faithfulness, that
I may have confidence in the Word of God, and true modesty and
chastity, that I may keep my body pure.

O Holy Spirit, help me keep my heart pure, that I may enjoy Your
friendship both now and in the glory of Your kingdom with the Fathe
and the Son. In Jesus' name. Amen.

Breathe in Me, O Holy Spirit
–Saint Augustine

Breathe in me, O Holy Spirit, that my thoughts may all be holy.
Act in me, O Holy Spirit, that my work, too, may be holy.
Draw my heart, O Holy Spirit, that I love but what is holy.
Strengthen me, O Holy Spirit, to defend all that is holy.
Guard me, then, O Holy Spirit, that I always may be holy. Amen.

Daily Consecration to the Holy Spirit

O Holy Spirit, divine Spirit of light and love, I consecrate to You my understanding, my heart and my will, my whole being, for time and eternity. May I always follow Your heavenly inspirations and the teachings of the Catholic Church, which You guide into all truth. May my heart be ever inflamed with love of God and others. May I conform my will to Your will, and may my whole life be a faithful imitation of the life and virtues of our Lord and Savior, Jesus Christ, to whom, with the Father and You, be honor and glory forever. Amen.

Prayer for the Indwelling of the Spirit

Holy Spirit, powerful Consoler, sacred Bond of the Father and the Son, Hope of the afflicted, come into my heart and establish Your Kingdom in me. Enkindle in me the fire of Your Love so that I may be wholly surrendered to You.

When You dwell in us, You also prepare a dwelling
for the Father and the Son. Please come to me,
Consoler of abandoned souls, and Protector of the needy.
Help the afflicted, strengthen the weak, and support the wavering.

Come and purify me. Let no evil desire take possession of me.
You love the humble and resist the proud.
Come to me, glory of the living and hope of the dying.
Lead me by Your grace that I may always be pleasing to You. Amen.

Prayer for the Outpouring of the Holy Spirit

Dear Spirit of Jesus, we ask for an outpouring of
Your graces, blessings and gifts,
upon those who do not believe,
that they may believe;
upon those who are doubtful or confused,
that they may understand;
upon those who are lukewarm or indifferent,
that they may be transformed;
upon those who are living in the state of sin,
that they may be converted;
upon those who are weak,
that they may be strengthened;
upon those who are holy,
that they may persevere.
Amen.

Prayer to Renew the Grace of My Confirmation

Dear Holy Spirit, thank You for coming into my heart in a special way on my Confirmation Day, when I was signed with sacred chrism and sealed with Your gift of grace. I praise, worship, and enjoy You! You make my soul Your home, You help me fight against evil, and You give me the victory won through Jesus' Passion, Death, and Resurrection.

O Holy Spirit, renew in me the grace of my Confirmation. Let me feel again Your love, peace, and joy. Forgive me for any ways I have grieved You or sinned against You, and give me the grace of a repentant and humble heart. Inflame me again with Your fire of love, O Holy Spirit, that I may be a light in this world. Help me witness by my life to Jesus' love, and in so doing, to lead others to Him.

I ask all this, dear Spirit of God, through the intercession of Mary, the Mother of Jesus and Your Spouse, for Your glory and the good of all humanity. Amen.

WHAT IS THE ROSARY?

When we pray, we speak to God, vocally or silently, and listen to Him in our hearts. He wants us to get to know and love Him. In the Rosary we pray to God with Mary, the Mother of Jesus, and our Mother as well. As we pray the prayers of the Rosary, we reflect on significant events, or mysteries, in the lives of Jesus and Mary. The complete Rosary consists of four groups of five mysteries each. These are the Joyful, Luminous, Sorrowful and Glorious Mysteries.

As we pray the Rosary, we try to imagine what was happening in each mystery and what God wants to teach us. We want to grow closer to Him and learn how He wants us to live. But even more, to pray the Rosary is to hold Mary's hand and let her bring us to Jesus. When we are with Jesus and Mary, we know the peace, love, and joy of God.

How to Pray the Rosary

- Begin by making the Sign of the Cross and praying *The Apostles' Creed* while you hold the crucifix.

- Pray one *Our Father* on the first bead, three *Hail Marys* on the next three beads for the virtues of Faith, Hope, and Charity, and finish with a *Glory Be*.

- Announce the first Mystery and think about it while praying an *Our Father* on the large bead, ten *Hail Marys* on the smaller beads, and finishing with a *Glory Be*. This is one decade.

- If you wish, you may add the *Fatima Prayer* after the *Glory Be:*

"O My Jesus, forgive us our sins, save us from the fires of hell. Lead all souls to heaven, especially those most in need of Your mercy."

Continue in this way until all you have prayed all five decades. To finish, pray the *Hail Holy Queen*.

Hail, Holy Queen

Hail, Holy Queen, Mother of Mercy,
our life, our sweetness, and our hope!
To thee do we cry, poor banished children of Eve;
to thee do we send up our sighs, mourning and weeping
in this valley of tears!
Turn then, most gracious Advocate, thine eyes of mercy
toward us; and after this, our exile, show unto us the
blessed fruit of thy womb, Jesus.
O clement,
O loving,
O sweet Virgin Mary.
V. Pray for us, O holy Mother of God.
R. That we may be made worthy
of the promises of Christ.

The Visitation

When Elizabeth heard Mary's greeting, the infant leaped in her womb, and Elizabeth, filled with the holy Spirit, cried out in a loud voice and said, "Most blessed are you among women, and blessed is the fruit of your womb."
–Luke 1:41-42

The Annunciation

Then the angel said to her, "Do not be afraid, Mary, for you have found favor with God. Behold, you will conceive in your womb and bear a son, and you shall name him Jesus."
–Luke 1:30-31

The Angel Gabriel told Mary that God had chosen her from all women to be the Mother of His Son. Mary said 'Yes' to God. Because of this, God could become man, and all people could be saved. Mary believed and trusted God even when it was hard to understand. She obeyed God, knowing He always works everything out for the good.

Dear Mother Mary, help us also say yes to God with a willing heart.

When Mary heard that her cousin Elizabeth was pregnant, she went quickly to visit and help her. Elizabeth was overjoyed to see Mary.

One of the best ways to make others happy is to visit them. In this way, we help bring the love of Jesus to others, just as Mary brought the love of Jesus to Elizabeth and her unborn child.

Dear Mother Mary, thank you for teaching us to be good to others. Help us always bring them joy, that they will feel the love of Jesus.

The Birth of Jesus

While they were there, the time came for her to have her child, and she gave birth to her firstborn son. She wrapped him in swaddling clothes and laid him in a manger, because there was no room for them in the inn.
–Luke 2:6-7

Long ago in Bethlehem, Mary gave birth to Jesus and laid Him in a manger. The angels sang, "Glory to God in the highest, and peace to His people on earth!"

Dear Mother Mary, help us to feel Jesus' love for us, and to love one another as well.

The Presentation of Jesus

"Now, Master, you may let your servant go in peace, according to your word, for my eyes have seen your salvation, which you prepared in sight of all the peoples, a light for revelation to the Gentiles, and glory for your people Israel."
–Luke 2:29-32

God promised Simeon that he would not die until he had seen the Messiah. God always keeps His promises, even when we have to wait a long time.

Dear Mother Mary, help us, like Simeon, trust that God will keep all His promises and bring us His salvation.

The Finding of Jesus

"Why were you looking for me? Did you not know that I must be in my Father's house?" But they did not understand what he said to them.
–Luke 2:49-50

Jesus always did His Father's Will, even when others did not understand. Nevertheless, He returned home with His parents and obeyed them.

Dear Mother Mary, help us to obey our parents, as Jesus did, and love God with all our hearts.

THE LUMINOUS MYSTERIES
Thursday

The Wedding at Cana

And when the headwaiter tasted the water that had become wine … the headwaiter called the bridegroom and said to him, "Everyone serves good wine first, and then when people have drunk freely, an inferior one; but you have kept the good wine until now."
–John 2:9-10

Jesus changed water into wine to serve others. In so doing, He revealed His glory. Mary teaches us in this mystery to do whatever her Son tells us.

Dear Mother Mary, when you asked Him, Jesus changed water into wine and opened the hearts of His followers to faith. Help me also trust in God in all that I do.

The Baptism of Jesus in the Jordan

After all the people had been baptized and Jesus also had been baptized and was praying, heaven was opened and the Holy Spirit descended upon him in bodily form like a dove. And a voice came from heaven, "You are my beloved Son; with you I am well pleased."
–Luke 3:21-22

Jesus obeyed His Father always, because he loved Him. Jesus teaches us to always begin our day with prayer, that we also may obey our Heavenly Father.

Dear Mother Mary, it is good to know my Heavenly Father loves me as He loves Jesus. Please pray that I will obey Him as Jesus did.

Jesus Proclaims God's Kingdom

After John had been arrested, Jesus came to Galilee proclaiming the gospel of God: "This is the time of fulfillment. The kingdom of God is at hand. Repent, and believe in the gospel." –Mark 1:14-15

Jesus proclaimed the good news that God was calling all people to come back to Him. We can only change our hearts with God's help.

Dear Mother Mary, help me to hear Jesus in His Word and in the quiet of my heart. Help me to obey Him and to love with His love.

The Transfiguration of Jesus

[Jesus] took Peter, John, and James and went up the mountain to pray. While he was praying, his face changed in appearance and his clothing became dazzling white. … Then from the cloud came a voice that said, "This is my chosen Son; listen to him."
–Luke 9:28-29, 35

Jesus calls us to be the light of the world. When we obey Jesus, His light shines through us. In this way we bring His light to everyone!

Dear Mother Mary, you always let the Lord shine His light in you and in your life. Help me listen to Jesus and let His light shine in my heart.

The Institution of the Eucharist

When the hour came, he … took the bread, said the blessing, broke it, and gave it to them, saying, "This is my body, which will be given for you; do this in memory of me." And he did the same with the cup after they had eaten, saying, "This cup is the new covenant in my blood, which will be shed for you."
–Luke 22:14, 19-20

Jesus loved us so much that He gave Himself so he could always be with us. May Mary help us always prepare a place for Jesus in our hearts.

Dear Mother Mary, thank you for sharing your Son with us so He could bring us His life. May we always be thankful for the gift of His Body and Blood.

THE SORROWFUL MYSTERIES
Tuesday, Friday

Jesus Is Scourged at the Pillar

So Pilate, wishing to satisfy the crowd, released Barabbas to them and, after he had Jesus scourged, handed him over to be crucified.
–Mark 15:15

The Agony in the Garden

*Then they came to a place called Gethsemane....
... And [Jesus] began to be troubled and distressed.*
–Mark 14:32-33

In the Garden of Gethsemane the night before He died, Jesus' friends fell asleep and He was all alone. He felt afraid, lonely, and very sad. Jesus prayed hard for His Father's help. Jesus placed all his trust and confidence in His Heavenly Father, as He had His whole life. Even when bad things happen, God will always take care of us.

Dear Mother Mary, please help me to remember Jesus and spend time with Him in prayer.

The soldiers arrested Jesus and put Him in prison. Pontius Pilate, who was afraid of the people, ordered the soldiers to whip Jesus even though He had done nothing wrong. The soldiers hurt Jesus very much. Yet during all this time, Jesus was thinking of us. He offered His suffering so we could someday come to heaven to be with Him forever.

Dear Mother Mary, please help me to love others even when they are not kind to me. May Jesus live in my heart today.

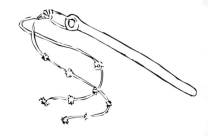

Jesus Is Crowned with Thorns

The soldiers wove a crown out of thorns and placed it on his head, and clothed him in a purple robe, and they came to him and said, "Hail, King of the Jews!"–John 19:2-3

The soldiers struck and mocked Jesus, but He suffered it all in silence. Jesus knew that one day His kingdom would surely come. He did not strike back at those who hurt Him, but offered His suffering up for them and for all people.

Dear Mother Mary, help me let Jesus love others through me.

Jesus Dies on the Cross

After they had crucified him, they divided his garments by casting lots; then they sat down and kept watch over him there.

–Matthew 27:35-36

As He hung on the cross, Jesus forgave His enemies. He gave us Mary to be our Mother, and gave us to Mary as her children. When everything was finished, Jesus bowed His head and died.

Dear Mother Mary, you were heartbroken when Jesus died, but you knew He did it for us. Thank you for sharing your Son with us all.

Jesus Carries the Cross

So they took Jesus, and carrying the cross by himself, he went out to what is called the Place of the Skull, which is called in Hebrew, Golgotha.

–John 19:16-17

Although Jesus was innocent, He took up His cross and carried it up the hill of Calvary. On the way the soldiers beat Him, and He fell under the cross. Jesus suffered for us, and gives us the strength to follow Him.

Dear Mary, you were very sad when you saw your Son carrying the cross. When He saw you He felt stronger. Help me assist others who may be hurting.

THE GLORIOUS MYSTERIES

Sunday, Wednesday

The Resurrection of Jesus

Then the angel said to the women in reply, "Do not be afraid! I know that you are seeking Jesus the crucified. He is not here, for he has been raised just as he said. Come and see the place where he lay."
–Matthew 28:5-6

After three days, Jesus arose from the dead! He won! He did it for us, so we could share in His victory over sin and death. Alleluia!

Dear Mother Mary, thank you for giving us your Son Jesus, who rose from the dead so we could always be with Him.

The Ascension of Jesus

As he blessed them, he parted from them and was taken up to heaven.
–Luke 24:51

Forty days after His Resurrection, Jesus gathered His disciples together. He told them to wait in Jerusalem until they received power from heaven. After Jesus blessed them, He was taken up into heaven.

Dear Mother Mary, help us to stay close to Jesus and bring His love to everyone.

The Descent of the Holy Spirit

When the time for Pentecost was fulfilled … suddenly there came from the sky a noise like a strong driving wind, and it filled the entire house in which they were. … And they were all filled with the holy Spirit. –Acts 2:1-4

On Pentecost, the Holy Spirit filled the disciples with faith and courage to bring God's love and forgiveness to all people.

Dear Mother Mary, you are filled with the Holy Spirit. Please pray that the Spirit will fill me with His fire of love. Amen.

The Assumption of Mary

Mary said: "My soul proclaims the greatness of the Lord; and my spirit rejoices in God my savior.…The Mighty One has done great things for me, and holy is his name."
–Luke 1:46-47, 49

Mary always said 'Yes' to God. God gave Mary a special gift at the end of her life. Jesus took His Mother, body and soul, to be in heaven with Him, forever.

Dear Mother Mary, please help me to love God that I may live forever with Him. Amen.

The Crowning of Mary

"He has helped his servant Israel, remembering his mercy."
–Luke 1:54-55

Adam and Eve disobeyed God, and lost His grace. Mary obeyed God, and through Jesus we have received God's grace back into our souls. Mary is our Heavenly Mother. She is very powerful and is always able to help us when we call on her.

Dear Mother Mary, please wrap us in your arms of love that we may always be close to God and bring others to rejoice in His salvation. In Jesus' Name. Amen!

THE STATIONS OF THE CROSS

On Good Friday, Jesus suffered and died to take away our sins. The Stations of the Cross help us remember the journey Jesus took to Calvary for our sake. At the beginning of each station, pray:

V. We adore You, O Christ, and we praise You.

R. Because by Your holy Cross, You have redeemed the world.

I. Jesus Is Condemned to Death

It was preparation day for Passover, and it was about noon. And he said to the Jews, "Behold, your king!" They cried out, "Take him away, take him away! Crucify him!" Pilate said to them, "Shall I crucify your king?" The chief priests answered, "We have no king but Caesar." Then he handed him over to them to be crucified. —John 19:14-16

After the Last Supper, Jesus went out with His disciples to the Garden of Gethsemane to pray. There He was betrayed by Judas, who brought soldiers to arrest Jesus. He was taken to prison, and the next day Pontius Pilate, the Roman Governor, had Jesus scourged and crowned with thorns. He knew Jesus was innocent but he was afraid of the crowds. So he condemned Jesus to die on the cross.

Jesus, when I am afraid, please help me to trust in You.

II. Jesus Accepts His Cross

Then he handed him over to them to be crucified. So they took Jesus, and carrying the cross himself he went out to what is called the Place of the Skull, in Hebrew, Golgotha. —John 19:16-17

Jesus saw the soldiers bringing the heavy cross for Him to carry. He was innocent, yet He chose to carry this cross for all of us, to set us free.

Jesus, teach me to obey God even when it is very hard, even when I am treated unfairly.

III. Jesus Falls for the First Time

We had all gone astray like sheep, each following his own way; But the LORD laid upon him the guilt of us all. —Isaiah 53:6

The cross was very heavy and Jesus was very weak after His beating. He fell under the cross and the soldiers beat Him until He stood up once again.

Jesus, teach me to keep going even when I feel like giving up. You are always with me.

IV. Jesus Meets His Mother Mary

Come, all you who pass by the way; look and see whether there is any suffering like my suffering.
—Lamentations 1:12

As Jesus struggled under the heavy cross, He looked into the crowd of angry people. Suddenly He saw His mother! How she wanted to hold Him and kiss Him and comfort Him! How He wanted to hold her and comfort her! Jesus and Mary looked at each other with great love, and then the soldiers pushed Him on his way.

Jesus, help me stay close to Mary, for then I will be close to You.

V. Simon Helps Jesus Carry the Cross

As they led him away they took hold of a certain Simon, a Cyrenian, who was coming in from the country; and after laying the cross on him, they made him carry it behind Jesus.
—Luke 23:26

The soldiers were afraid that Jesus would die before they reached Calvary. So they pulled a man out of the crowd, laid the cross on him, and made him carry it behind Jesus.

Help me, Jesus, to help those who need me.

VI. Veronica Wipes the Face of Jesus

He was spurned and avoided by men, a man of suffering, accustomed to infirmity. —Isaiah 53:3

All His life, Jesus had helped other people. Now, in His time of trouble, a woman named Veronica reached out to wipe His face. She felt afraid of the soldiers but she helped Jesus anyway. She dried away the sweat and blood, and Jesus was very thankful.

Jesus, help me to be not afraid to do good.

VII. Jesus Falls a Second Time

I was hard pressed and falling, but the LORD came to my help.
—Psalm 118:13

Jesus was growing weaker and weaker. He wanted to keep going but His legs gave way beneath Him and He fell a second time. The crowd laughed at Him and shoved Him as He struggled to get up and keep going. Still He loved them all.

Jesus, help me to follow You even when others laugh at me.

VIII. Jesus Meets the Women of Jerusalem

"Daughters of Jerusalem, do not weep for me; weep instead for yourselves and for your children."
—Luke 23:28

Some women from Jerusalem came out, crying, to meet Jesus. Jesus told them to weep instead for themselves and their children, because if the Son of God had to suffer so much, what would happen to those who turned away from Him?

Jesus, help me stay close to You.

IX. Jesus Falls the Third Time

He humbled himself, becoming obedient to death, even death on a cross. —Philippians 2:8

As Jesus climbed the hill of Calvary, He fell one last time. He could hardly lift His head. Yet Jesus knew He had to die for us on the cross, so with one final effort He got up and finished His journey.

Jesus, Your love for us kept You going. Help me to believe in Your love for me and to always get up when I make mistakes.

X. Jesus Is Stripped of His Garments

They divide my garments among them;
for my clothing they cast lots. —Psalm 22:19

Finally Jesus came to the top of Mount Calvary. The soldiers stripped his clothes off Him, and prepared to nail Him to the cross. Jesus allowed them to do this to Him because He loved you and me.

Jesus, help me be strong when others are weak.

XI. Jesus Is Nailed to the Cross

When they came to the place called
the Skull, they crucified him and the
criminals there, one on his right,
the other on his left.
—Luke 23:33

The soldiers nailed Jesus' hands and feet to the cross. Then they raised the cross up so everyone could see Him. Jesus hung there in front of the crowd, loving them even as they crucified Him.

Jesus, help me be silent when I feel like complaining.

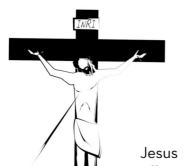

XII. Jesus Dies Upon the Cross

Jesus cried out in a loud voice, "Father, into your hands I commend my spirit"; and when he had said this he breathed his last.
—Luke 23:46

Jesus hung on the cross for three hours. He offered his suffering for all of us, that we might be able to enter heaven and enjoy eternal life with God. He died so we could have the power to love one another as He loved us. In the end, Jesus won the battle over sin and death.

Jesus, thank You for dying for us. Thank You for giving us the grace to be free from sin. Help us to follow You always.

XIII. Jesus Is Taken Down from the Cross

They shall look on him whom they have thrust through, and they shall mourn for him as one mourns for an only son.
—Zechariah 12:10

Jesus' friends gently took Him off the cross, and placed His body in the arms of Mary. Mary used to rock Jesus gently in her arms and sing to Him when He was a little baby. Now as she cradled Him again, only God knew the sorrow in her heart.

Mary, sometimes I am very sad, too. Help me remember you are always near, and you will hold me as you held your only Son.

XIV. Jesus Is Placed in the Tomb

They took the body of Jesus and bound it with burial cloths along with the spices ....
They laid Jesus there because of the Jewish preparation day; for the tomb was close by.
—John 19:40, 42

Jesus was born in a stable that belonged to someone else and buried in a tomb not His own. His mother Mary and His friends washed His body and covered it with spices and clean cloths. Then they rolled a great stone over the entrance to the tomb.

Jesus, I trust in You.

XV. Jesus Rises from the Dead

He said to them, "Do not be amazed! You seek Jesus of Nazareth, the crucified. He has been raised; he is not here. Behold, the place where they laid him." —Mark 16:6

The tomb could not hold Jesus! On the third day, just as He said, Jesus rose from the dead. A new light of joy and peace dawned in Mary's heart and in the hearts of His disciples.

Jesus, I receive Your Resurrection Life in my heart today!

THE HOLY SPIRIT DESCENDS UPON THE APOSTLES

After Jesus ascended into heaven, the apostles returned to Jerusalem. Mother Mary was with them, as were many other followers of Jesus. There were about 120 disciples gathered together. As they waited there in an upper room, the apostles prayed with great fervor. They waited and prayed, as Jesus had told them to do.

Then, a few days later, it was time to celebrate the Jewish feast of Harvest. The name of the feast was Pentecost. When the day of Pentecost arrived, all the disciples were united together. Suddenly there came from heaven a noise like a strong driving wind. The wind filled the whole room where they were sitting. There appeared tongues as of fire, which parted and came to rest on each one of them. Every one of the disciples was filled with the Holy Spirit. They began to speak in different tongues, as the Spirit enabled them to proclaim.

Now at that time, there were prayerful Jews from every nation staying in Jerusalem. They had come there to celebrate the feast of Pentecost. When they heard the sounds coming from where Mary and the disciples were gathered, the people collected in a large crowd around the room. They were confused because each one heard the apostles speaking in his own language.

The Jews asked in amazement, "Are not all these people who are speaking from Galilee? Then how does each one of us hear them speaking in our own native language? We have come to Jerusalem from all over the world. Some of us are from Arabia and Asia. Other are from Rome and Greece. Still others of us are from far away, in Africa. Yet we hear these men and women speaking in our own languages, praising the mighty works of God."

PETER PREACHES AT PENTECOST

All the people who heard the disciples speaking in other languages were surprised and puzzled. They said to one another, "What does this mean?" But others said, "They have had too much new wine."

Peter stood up with the apostles and proclaimed in a loud voice to all the people, "You who are Jews, indeed all of you staying in Jerusalem. Listen to my words, for I have something very important to tell you. These people are not drunk, as you suppose, for it is only nine o'clock in the morning. No, this is what was spoken through the prophet Joel long ago.

"In the Scripture, Joel wrote this: 'It will come to pass in the last days,' says the Lord, 'that I will pour out a portion of my spirit upon all people. Your sons and your daughters shall prophesy. Your young men shall see visions, and your old men shall dream dreams. Indeed, upon my servants and my handmaids I will pour out a portion of my spirit in those days, and they shall prophesy.'"

The Lord continued, "I will work wonders in the heavens above and signs on the earth below: blood, fire, and a cloud of smoke. The sun shall be turned to darkness, and the moon to blood, before the coming of the great and splendid day of the Lord, and it shall come to pass that everyone who calls on the name of the Lord shall be saved."

Peter said, "Jesus of Nazareth was a man whom God gave to you with mighty deeds, wonders, and signs. God worked these through Jesus while He lived among you, as you yourselves know. Yet you killed this man, using men who did not know the Law to crucify Him."

Peter continued, "However, God raised Jesus. We are all witnesses. Therefore let all the Jewish people know for certain that God has made this Jesus whom you crucified both Lord and Messiah."

When the people heard this, they felt very sad and guilty in their hearts. They asked Peter and the other apostles, "What are we to do, brothers?" Peter said to them, "Repent and be baptized, every one of you, in the name of Jesus Christ for the forgiveness of your sins, and you will receive the gift of the Holy Spirit." He cried, "Save yourselves from this wicked generation." Three thousand people accepted Peter's message and were baptized that day. The Church was born!

PETER PREACHES TO CORNELIUS

In Caesarea there was a centurion named Cornelius, a devout man who loved God along with his whole household. He sent men to Peter, who said, "We come on behalf of Cornelius, a centurion in Caesarea. He is an upright and good man. He loves God and he is respected by the whole Jewish nation. A holy angel appeared to him and told him to invite you to his house and to hear what you have to say."

When Peter heard this, he invited the men in and welcomed them. The next day Peter got up and went with the men, along with some of the believers from Joppa. When they arrived in Caesarea, Cornelius was waiting for them. He had called together his family, relatives and close friends. When Peter entered the home, Cornelius met him and fell down at his feet in respect. Peter, however, raised him up. He said to Cornelius, "Get up. I myself am also a human being." Peter then said to the many people gathered together there, "It is unlawful for a Jewish man to visit a Gentile. However,

God has shown me I should not call unclean what He has made clean. That is the reason I came to you when you invited me to do so. Now, may I ask why you sent for me?"

Cornelius told Peter about the angel who had appeared to him and had told him to send for Peter. Cornelius said, "Thank you for coming to us. Now, we are all here in the presence of God to listen to all that you have been commanded by the Lord." Peter said, "In truth, I see that God does not prefer one person over another. Rather, in every nation whoever worships Him and acts in a right way is acceptable to Him."

Peter then preached about Jesus to Cornelius and all his family and friends. While Peter was still speaking, the Holy Spirit came upon all who heard, and they began to speak in tongues, and to praise God. Then Peter said, "Can anyone forbid baptism for these people? After all, they have received the Holy Spirit even as we have!" All of the people were then baptized. In this way God showed that Jesus had come to bring salvation to all people, both Jews and Gentiles. Truly Jesus was the Lord of all.

Q & A ON CATHOLIC DOCTRINE
God Reveals Himself

Humanity hungers for God! Because He created us for Himself, no one and nothing else will do. Only in God will we find the truth and happiness we incessantly seek. Our dignity rests above all in the fact that God has called us to communion with Himself.

1. Who is God?

God is love, and whoever remains in love
remains in God and God in him.
–1 John 4:16

The Catholic Church believes and professes that there is one true, living God, the Creator and Lord of heaven and earth. He is almighty, eternal, beyond measure, incomprehensible, and infinite in intellect, will and in every perfection.

2. How did God call a people of faith to Himself?

True to His Word, God called Abram from home and country, changing his name to Abraham, "father of many nations." From Abraham's descendants God brought forth a people, Israel, with whom He established a covenant and through Moses, gave them His Law. Israel sought to follow God but continually failed Him. Still, God prepared them through the prophets for the salvation that would deliver all humanity. Holy men and women kept Israel's faith and hope alive, but especially Mary of Nazareth, the purest of them all.

But when the fullness of time had come, God sent his Son, born of
a woman, born under the law, to ransom those under the law,
so that we might receive adoption.
–Galatians 4:4-5

Christ, the Son of God become man through the Virgin Mary, is the Father's unique, perfect, and final Word. He is the "gift of the Father." There will be no further Revelation. Public Revelation is complete but not completely explicit; it remains to be grasped over the centuries.

3. How did God pass on His Revelation?

"God ... wills everyone to be saved and to come to knowledge of the truth" (1 Timothy 2:3-4). Jesus commanded His apostles to preach th

Gospel to the whole world. The apostles spread the Gospel orally, through their preaching, example and institutions. They and their associates also spread it in writing, under the inspiration of the Holy Spirit.

4. Who are the successors of the Apostles?

The Bishops teach with the authority of the Apostles, whom they succeed. This living transmission is called Apostolic Tradition. Through Tradition, "the Church, in her doctrine, life, and worship perpetuates and transmits to every generation all that she herself is, all that she believes." (*CCC #78*)

5. How is Sacred Tradition connected to the Scriptures?

Sacred Tradition and Sacred Scriptures, the "speech of God" written under the direction of the Holy Spirit, are bound closely together. Each of them makes present in the Church the mystery of Christ, who has promised never to forsake us.

The task of interpreting Scripture and Tradition has been entrusted to the Magisterium, consisting of the bishops in communion with the pope.

By virtue of their Baptism, the faithful have received the anointing of the Holy Spirit to help them understand and share these truths. Through their faith the People of God welcome, study, and live more fully the truths of Divine Revelation.

6. How does the Lord help us understand His revelation?

If the Scriptures are to remain alive, Christ Jesus must, through the Holy Spirit, open our minds to understand them. We need to read God's Word within the living Tradition of the Church.

The Gospels are the heart of Scripture, because they are our principal source of the life and teaching of Jesus.

7. What does the Church tell us about reading the Scriptures?

The Church compellingly urges us to read Scripture frequently. In the immortal words of Saint Jerome, "Ignorance of the Scriptures is ignorance of Christ."

8. On whose authority do we believe?

We believe on God's authority, yet we seek understanding. Faith in Jesus, the One sent from the Father, is necessary for salvation.

9. Where are the articles of our faith contained?

The Church professes a common faith expressed in the Apostles' Creed, the oldest Roman Catechism, and the Nicene Creed. (See page 46.)

Let's take a look together at its articles.

I. I Believe in God, the Father Almighty

God the Father is the first Person of the Most Holy Trinity. God revealed Himself to Israel as the one God. Jesus affirmed that, yet revealed that He Himself was "the Lord," and that the Holy Spirit was also God. The Trinity, then, is One God in Three Persons, each of them distinct from the other, yet God whole and entire.

10. To whom does God want to communicate the glory of His blessed life?

God wants to communicate the glory of His blessed life to all. He destined us in love to be His children, to be conformed to the image of His Son. (See Ephesians 1:4-5; Romans 8:29.) That's why He made us, saved us, and continues His mission today in the Church. The ultimate purpose of God's work is to bring us into the union of the Blessed Trinity, for whom even now we are called to be a dwelling-place in the Spirit.

11. What kind of power does God have?

God holds universal power—the power of love, for He is our Father. His power is mysteriously "made perfect in weakness" (2 Corinthians 12:9). As Lord of the Universe and Lord of History, God takes care of us and forgives our sins out of His infinite mercy. Only by faith can we embrace God, for whom nothing is impossible!

II. Creator of Heaven and Earth

In the beginning…God created the heavens and the earth.
–Genesis 1:1

12. Where do we come from?

Creation is the foundation of God's saving plan, the beginning of salvation history whose culmination is Christ Himself. Beyond the natural knowledge we could have of the Creator, from Scripture we learn of the creation and fall of our first parents, and of God's promise of salvation. God created everything out of nothing, through His Son, His eternal Word, and the Holy Spirit.

13. Why did God create the world?

God made the world to show forth and communicate His glory. His ultimate purpose is to at last become "all in all," assuring at the same time His glory and our beatitude.

14. What did God create first?

God created the angels, pure spirits who serve as His messengers, serving Him and guarding each of us.

15. If a good God created the world, why is there evil?

Satan, whose power is real but not infinite, was originally a good angel who with the other fallen angels 'radically and irrevocably" rejected God and His reign. He tempted Adam and Eve to disobey God and eat from the tree of the knowledge of good and evil. Immediately they lost the grace of original holiness and fellowship with God. The shadow of death entered human history.

16. Why does God permit evil?

God permits evil because He has given to angels and humans the power of free choice. Sin brings with it the consequences of physical and moral evil, and ultimately death. Still God is able to work all things out for the good.

17. Even with Original Sin, do we still have dignity?

God created our first parents, Adam and Eve, in His friendship, and continues to create every person as the summit of His creation in the world, with great worth and dignity. Moreover, we are all in solidarity with one another. God created man and woman for union with each other as equal human persons. Their original holiness, justice, and happiness flowed from their friendship with Him.

18. Is there hope for liberation?

Thankfully, God did not abandon us but promised a Redeemer, who would win a definitive victory for all humanity. Jesus Christ's triumph over sin has given us greater blessings than those lost by our first parents. Baptism removes original sin, with which we are all born, and turns us back towards God. However, our weakened nature and inclination to sin—concupiscence—remains. All of our life is a spiritual battle.

In summary, God created the world from nothing and keeps it in existence out of love. Humanity fell into slavery because of sin, but by His death and resurrection Christ Jesus set us free and broke the power of sin. To God be the glory!

III. And in Jesus Christ, His Only Son Our Lord

But when the fullness of time had come, God sent his Son, born of a woman, born under the law, to ransom those under the law, so that we might receive adoption. –Galatians 4:4-5

God fulfilled His promise to us by sending His only Son. We proclaim with Peter that Jesus is "the Christ, the Son of the living God," that we might lead others to faith in Him. Only He can lead us to the Father and into our destined life in the Holy Trinity.

19. What does the name "Jesus" mean?

Jesus—*Yeshua*—means "God saves." Since God alone can forgive sins, it is only Jesus who can save His people from their sins. "There is no salvation through anyone else, nor is there any other name under heaven given to the human race by which we are to be saved" (Acts 4:12).

20. What does the word "Christ" mean?

Christ—*Messiah*—means "Anointed One." Jesus, anointed priest, prophet, and king by the Holy Spirit, revealed His true kingship on the Cross. After the Resurrection, Peter boldly proclaimed, "Therefore let the whole house of Israel know for certain that God has made him both Lord and Messiah, this Jesus whom you crucified" (Acts 2:36).

Lord—*Yahweh*—is the holy name of God. The New Testament uses this title for the Father and for Jesus, thus affirming that the power, honor, and glory due to God the Father are due also to Jesus, His beloved Son.

IV. He Was Conceived by the Power of the Holy Spirit

The Word became flesh to save us from our sins and reconcile us to God, to be our model of holiness, and to make us partakers of the divine nature. As Saint Athanasius said, "For the Son of God became man so that we might become God." That's how much God loves us!

21. Is Jesus true God and true man?

Yes. From the beginning, the Church had to defend this awesome, mysterious, and hard-to-believe truth from heresies that tried to falsely explain it away. In 431 AD, the Council of Ephesus proclaimed that Mary truly became the Mother of God by the human conception of the Son of God through the power of the Holy Spirit in her womb. The Church thus proclaims that Jesus Christ is true God and true man at the same time.

> "For, by His incarnation, He, the Son of God, has in a certain way united Himself with each man. He worked with human hands, He thought with a human mind. He acted with a human will, and with a human heart He loved. Born of the Virgin Mary, He has truly been made one of us, like to us in all things except sin." (*Pastoral Constitution On The Church In The Modern World*, par. 22).

22. How was Jesus true God and true man?

Jesus had a human soul fused to His divine nature. As such, His human knowledge expressed His divine inner life. For example, Jesus always had an intimate knowledge of His Heavenly Father. As a man, Jesus knew what only God could know, and as God He experienced what only man could experience. Jesus' Sacred Heart, pierced on the Cross, is ever the sign of His love for His Father and each one of us—a love that will stop at nothing to draw us to Himself.

V. And Born of the Virgin Mary

In the Annunciation to Mary, God initiated the fulfillment of His promises. Desiring our free cooperation, God chose from all eternity a virgin daughter of Israel to be the mother of His Son. Just as a woman shared in the Fall of humanity, so should a woman share in our Redemption.

23. How did God prepare Mary for her unique role in the redemption of the world?

God enriched Mary with gifts appropriate to her role, blessing her more than any other created person. Mary was conceived without Original Sin through the merits of Jesus Christ, and by God's grace remained free of any personal sin her entire life.

24. How did Mary respond to God's initiative?

Mary accepted God's invitation and became the mother of Jesus, thus reversing in her obedience the disobedience of Eve. The Holy Spirit overshadowed Mary, sanctifying her womb and implanting the divine seed, causing her to conceive God's Son in her humanity. The Church thus confesses that Mary is truly "Mother of God."

25. How did Jesus reveal the Father?

Jesus revealed the Father in His whole life. Everything He did, said, and suffered was done to restore us to our original vocation—to live as the children of God. Christ Jesus enables us to live in Him all that He lived, and He lives it in us.

26. How did Jesus relate to Mary and Joseph?

Jesus Christ's obedience to Joseph and Mary fulfilled the fourth commandment and anticipated His obedience to His Father in His Passion. Jesus spent most of His life as a laborer, without any evident greatness, as a Jew obedient to the Law of God, so everyone could relate to Him in the most ordinary events of daily life.

27. When did Jesus begin His public ministry?

In His Baptism in the Jordan, Jesus was manifested as Messiah of Israel and Son of God. Afterwards, just as Adam was tempted in Paradise and Israel was tempted in the desert, so was Jesus tempted. He was faithful to God and the devil left Him "until an opportune time."

28. What did Jesus preach?

Jesus preached, "This is the time of fulfillment. The kingdom of God is at hand. Repent, and believe in the gospel" (Mark 1:15). He performed many mighty works, signs, and wonders, to free us from our slavery to sin, which thwarts us in our vocation as the children of God, and He invited all people to faith.

29. What did Jesus do in His ministry?

The coming of God's Kingdom meant the defeat of Satan's rule. Jesus chose twelve apostles to assist Him in His mission and He gave them

His authority. The chief of these was Peter, to whom Jesus gave the keys of the Kingdom of Heaven. When His final Passover drew near, Jesus set His face toward Jerusalem. He entered the city in humility, seated on a donkey, yet manifesting a Kingdom to come through His Passion, Death, and Resurrection—a Kingdom of Love.

VI. Jesus Christ Suffered under Pontius Pilate

But now once for all he has appeared at the end of the ages to take away sin by his sacrifice.
–Hebrews 9:26

30. Why did Jesus have to die?

God's saving plan was finally realized by the death of His Son Jesus Christ for the redemption of all. From the beginning, certain religious leaders of Israel agreed to destroy Jesus. His expulsion of demons, forgiveness of sins, and healing on the Sabbath led to suspicions of demonic possession and more serious accusations of blasphemy and false prophecy, punishable by death.

31. How did Jesus respond to the charges against Him?

Jesus was faithful to the Law, the Temple, and Israel's faith in the One God and Savior. When He forgave sins, the Pharisees were scandalized, since only God could forgive sins. The leadership of Israel tragically misunderstood Jesus, out of ignorance and the hardness of their unbelief.

32. Who is responsible for Jesus' death?

The Jews are not collectively responsible for Jesus' death. In truth, all humanity is responsible, since it was our sins that crucified Christ. Even so, Jesus was handed over according to the definite plan of God, who allows our free choices and still accomplishes His Will. Jesus took upon Himself our sins, so that we might be reconciled to God. The Father did not spare His own Son but gave Him up for us all, to reconcile us to God.

33. Did Jesus die for everyone?

To sum up, Jesus Christ suffered and died for every human being, without exception. He offered Himself freely, out of love for His Father, to give His life as a ransom for many.

VII. Was Crucified, Died, and Was Buried

On the night He was betrayed, while still free, Jesus gave us His Body and Blood, a memorial of His imminent sacrifice. Jesus instituted His apostles as priests of the New Covenant, commanding them to perpetuate the memorial as the Eucharist.

34. What does the Death of Jesus do for us?

Jesus' death is the Paschal sacrifice that redeems us and is the sacrifice of the New Covenant, which restores us to communion with God. It is a gift from God the Father, who gave His Son to reconcile us to Himself. It is the offering of Jesus, who freely offered His life to make reparation for our disobedience. It is Christ's loving obedience to His Father and utterly selfless love for each of us that gives His sacrifice its redemptive and reparative value.

35. What does Jesus offer us in His death?

Jesus offers to each of us the possibility of participating in the Paschal Mystery, calling us to daily take up our cross and follow Him. Jesus tasted death for everyone. This is the mystery of the tomb and descent into hell. On Holy Saturday, Christ reveals God's great Sabbath rest, after fulfilling our salvation and bringing peace to the whole universe.

36. What happened to Jesus when He died?

Death put an end to Jesus' earthly existence, separating His soul from His body, as it does to every person. Christ's divine power, however, preserved His body from corruption.
(See Psalm 16:9-10.)

VIII. He Descended into Hell and on the Third Day He Rose Again

(Jesus)... descended into the lower [regions] of the earth ... the one who ascended far above all the heavens. —Ephesians 4:9-10

37. Where did Jesus go after He died on the cross?

Jesus went to the abode of the dead to proclaim the Word of Life. Scripture calls this abode "hell," whose inhabitants are deprived of the vision of God. Jesus descended to liberate the righteous souls imprisoned there. "He has gone to search for Adam, our first father, is for a lost sheep.... **I did not create you to be a prisoner in hell. Rise from the dead, for I am the life of the dead."** —*Ancient Homily for Holy Saturday.*

88. When did Jesus rise from the dead?

On the third day, Jesus Christ, the Son of God made man, the Crucified One, rose from the dead! The Resurrection is the crowning truth of our Christian faith, to which the New Testament, the empty tomb, and our living Tradition, all bear witness. Mary Magdalene and the holy women first encountered the risen Lord, followed by Peter, the Apostles, and many more.

89. What type of body did Jesus have when He rose from the dead?

Jesus did not return to earthly life, but rose with a Spirit-filled, glorified body: "the man from heaven," according to Saint Paul. The Resurrection proves Jesus' divinity, fulfilling the Messianic prophecies and confirming Christ's words and works. By His death and resurrection, Christ liberates us from sin and opens the way for a new life. This new life is a victory over the death of sin and a justification that reinstates us in God's grace. What is more, it is a promise of our own future resurrection!

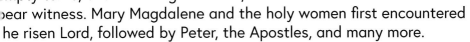

IX. He Ascended into Heaven and Is Seated at the Right Hand of the Father. From Thence He Shall Come to Judge the Living and the Dead.

So then the Lord Jesus, after he spoke to them, was taken up into heaven and took his seat at the right hand of God. —Mark 16:19

At His Ascension, Christ's humanity was irreversibly taken up into divine glory, and He is now seated bodily at the right hand of the Father, where He lives to forever intercede for us, thus assuring the permanent outpouring of the Spirit. As High Priest, Christ leads the heavenly worship in honor of the Father, and gives us hope of someday joining Him there.

40. How does Christ Jesus now dwell with us?

Already reigning from heaven, Christ now dwells on earth in His Church, where the Kingdom is present in mystery. His reign is destined to be filled with power and great glory when He returns to earth. Until then, the present is a time of Spirit and witness, distress and trial, for the world and the Church.

41. What needs to happen before Christ Jesus returns in glory?

Before Christ returns, Israel must recognize and accept its Messiah, and the Church must pass through a final trial that will test and purify many. A religious deception will appear, offering a solution to all problems in return for apostasy. The Church will enter the glory of the Kingdom only through this final purifying Passover.

Then comes the Last Judgement, when Christ will reveal the secrets of all hearts and give to each of us according to our works and our acceptance or refusal of His grace.

X. I Believe in the Holy Spirit

The Holy Spirit must first touch us if we are to touch Christ. We encounter the Spirit in the Scriptures, Tradition, Magisterium, and liturgy of the Church, as well as in its charisms and ministries, in the signs of apostolic and missionary life, the witness of the saints, and in prayer. The Spirit unites us to Christ and makes us live in Him.

XI. I Believe in the Holy Catholic Church

The Church—*Ecclesia*—is the assembly of the believers, the People of God, "the place where the Spirit flourishes" (Saint Hippolytus).

42. How did Jesus inaugurate the Church?

Jesus inaugurated the Church by preaching the reign of God. He gathered around him a little flock, teaching them a new way of acting and praying, and giving them a structure to remain until the Kingdom fully comes, with the Apostles, led by Peter, as its foundation stones.

43. What is the "soul" of the Church?

The Holy Spirit is the "soul" of the Church, giving her gifts and charisms to help her make disciples of all nations. She is to proclaim and establish among all the kingdom of God, of which she is the seed and beginning. The Church, after enduring great trials, will reach perfection at Christ's return. Until then, she continues her pilgrimage in persecution and consolation.

44. What is the nature of the Church?

The Church is both human and divine, the "mystery of salvation" through which Christ is loving, teaching, saving, and sanctifying all who come to Him. As members of Christ we have the dignity and freedom of the children of God. Called to be salt of the earth and light of the world, we are to love as Christ loved us. Our destiny is the Kingdom of God.

45. How does Saint Paul compare the union of Christ Jesus and the Church?

Saint Paul compares the union of Christ and the Church to the conjugal union of a bride and bridegroom. Mary is the sign of what we shall someday be, a bride without spot or wrinkle. Saint Augustine proclaims, "Let us rejoice...that we have become not only Christians, but Christ himself."

46. What are the four marks of the Catholic Church?

Christ, through the Holy Spirit, makes His Church **one, holy, catholic, and apostolic.** These characteristics point out four essential facets of the Church and her mission.

47. How is the Church one?

The Church is one because God, her source, is one. The Church also has a great diversity, as all peoples and cultures are one in her. The Church is united by its profession of one faith received from the Apostles, by its common celebration of divine worship, and by the apostolic succession.

48. What about the Christians who are not Catholic?

The Church accepts with respect and affection as brothers and sisters those Christians separated from the Catholic Church, even as she prays with Christ that all may be one. Finally, over all these things, we are to "put on love, which is the bond of perfection" (Colossians 3:14).

49. How is the Church holy?

The Church is holy, because Christ loved her as His Bride, gave Himself up to sanctify her, joined her to Himself as His Body, and gave her the gift of the Holy Spirit. The members of the People of God are called saints. The vocation of every Christian is to be holy, to love, with Mary as our "all-holy" model.

50. How is the Church catholic?

The Church is catholic (universal) first of all because Christ is present in her in His fullness and has given her the fullness of the means of salvation. As Saint Ignatius of Antioch said, "Where there is Christ Jesus, there is the Catholic Church."

The Church is catholic secondly because Christ has sent her to the whole human race. The Church is "the world reconciled." All salvation comes from Christ, the Head, through the Church, His Body. Those too, who through no fault of their own, seek God without knowing His Gospel, may also achieve eternal salvation.

51. How is the Church apostolic?

The Church is apostolic: she was founded on the Apostles, hands on the apostolic teaching; and continues to be shepherded by the bishops, successors of the Apostles, headed by the successor of Peter. In the Church there is a diversity of ministry but unity of mission: the salvation of the world.

52. Who is the head of the Church on earth?

The Pope, successor of Saint Peter, is the visible foundation of Christ's Church. He enjoys supreme, full, immediate, and universal power in the care of souls. Bishops, priests, and deacons assist him in this office. The laity who live in the world minister as priests, prophets, and kings.

XII. I Believe in the Communion of Saints

They devoted themselves to the teaching of the apostles and to the communal life, to the breaking of the bread and to the prayers.
–Acts 2:42

From her birth, the Church has been a communion of saints—holy people who share holy things. We share together our faith, the sacraments, (especially Eucharist), spiritual charisms, and love. Jesus calls us to share our material goods as well, especially with those in need. Our acts of love benefit everyone, while our sins harm all.

53. What do we mean by the communion of saints?

We share a communion with the saints in heaven, relying on their intercession, as well as with the dead, praying for them to be freed from their sins. Here on earth we are called to love one another, fulfilling our deepest vocation as Christians.

54. How are we related to the Virgin Mary?

Mary, Mother of Christ, is also Mother of the Church, as Saint Augustine said, "since she by her charity joined in bringing about the birth of believers in the Church." From the cross, Jesus entrusted all of us to Mary, our spiritual mother.

55. How does our Mother Mary assist us?

At Pentecost, Mary implored the gift of the Holy Spirit upon the Apostles. Her Assumption anticipates our own Resurrection from the dead. As our model of faith and love, Mother Mary is truly *Help of Christians*. The Church honors Mary with special devotion, fulfilling her prophecy that "all generations will call me blessed" (Luke 1:48). Mary is a sign of what we as Church shall someday be, with her help and through her intercession: the spotless Bride of Christ.

XIII. I Believe in the Forgiveness of Sins, the Resurrection of the Body

Baptism unites us with Christ Jesus and cleanses us from all sin; however, our tendency to sin, our concupiscence, remains. Therefore, we need to be forgiven. The Sacrament of Penance, a great and merciful gift, reconciles us to God and the Church, no matter how serious the offense.

56. What happens to us after death?

After death our bodies decay and our souls go to meet God. We believe that, just as Christ truly is resurrected from the dead, so also Christ's faithful ones shall live forever with Him, and He will raise up their bodies on the last day. Jesus said, "I am the resurrection and the life; whoever believes in me, even if he dies, will live" (John 11:25).

57. In what way do we already share in Christ's risen life?

In a certain way, believers have already risen with Christ and participate in His risen life, a life that is "hidden with Christ in God." (See Colossians 3:3; also Colossians 2:12.) As we partake of the Eucharist, we already eat the bread of heaven, for Jesus promised, "Whoever eats my flesh and drinks my blood <u>has</u> eternal life, and I will raise him on the last day" (John 6:54; emphasis added).

58. What is the end of our earthly existence?

Death, the ultimate consequence of sin, is the end of our earthly pilgrimage. We each have only a limited time to accomplish God's Will for us. Thankfully, Jesus' obedience in accepting death for all of us has transformed the curse of death into a blessing. We can follow Christ's example and transform our own death into an act of love towards God as well. Thus the Church calls us to prepare now for the hour of our death.

XIV. And Life Everlasting

Death ends human life as the time open to either accepting or rejecting God's grace; there is no reincarnation. At the moment of death, each person receives his or her particular judgement— entrance into heaven, purgatory, or hell.

59. How shall we be judged after our death?

Saint John of the Cross wrote, "At the evening of our life, we shall be judged on love alone." Those who die in God's grace and are perfectly purified will see God face to face in heaven, the fulfillment of our deepest longing and a state of absolute bliss. Heaven is a communion of life and love with the Trinity, Mother Mary, the angels, and all the blessed.

60. What is purgatory?

Purgatory is the place of final purification for all who die in God's grace but are imperfectly purified. We can by our prayers and sacrifices help relieve the souls in purgatory and move them more quickly into heaven.

61. What is hell?

To die in mortal sin without repentance, rejecting God's all-merciful love, is to choose forever to be in hell. Jesus warns repeatedly of the fires of Gehenna. The Church calls us to responsibility and conversion, for God neither desires nor predestines anyone to go to hell.

62. When will the dead in Christ rise again?

The resurrection of the dead will precede the Last Judgement. Christ will return in glory, ushering in the Kingdom of God. The righteous will reign with Christ, and there will be "a new heaven and a new earth" (Revelation 21:1).

XV. Amen

Amen, the final word of the Creed, means I believe, I agree, with the faithful God and His Gospel of peace.

The Liturgy as Celebration

63. Who leads us in worship?

Christ Jesus Himself unceasingly leads heavenly worship, with Mary and the holy ones. We also, as sharers in His priesthood, celebrate liturgy on earth. Nourished by this encounter, we go forth to be Christ to our world.

64. What does the Church call us to in worship?

The Church calls us to full, conscious, and active participation in worship. We hear God's Word proclaimed and respond in faith. We worship the Lord in song and music. Sacred images nourish our faith as we venerate the persons they represent.

65. How do we keep holy the Lord's Day?

Sunday, the Lord's Day, is our central day as the Body of Christ to celebrate the Eucharist, enjoy our loved ones, and rest from work. Beginning in Advent, the Church unfolds throughout the year the whole mystery of Christ, remembering as well Mary and the saints.

Sacraments and Sacramentals

The seven sacraments of Baptism, Confirmation (Chrismation), Eucharist, Penance, Anointing of the Sick, Holy Orders, and Matrimony are the center of the entire liturgical life of the Church. These are powers that come forth from the Body of Christ, actions of the Holy Spirit, and masterworks of God.

66. Who benefits from the sacraments?

Sacraments benefit the whole Church and sanctify the person receiving them. They build up the Body of Christ and give worship to God. The ordained clergy guarantees that it is Christ Jesus who acts in His sacraments.

67. How is a sacrament a sign?

"A sacrament is a sign that commemorates what precedes it—Christ's Passion; demonstrates what is accomplished in us through Christ's Passion—grace; and prefigures what that Passion pledges to us—future glory." –Saint Thomas Aquinas

68. What is a sacramental?

Sacramentals are sacred signs instituted by the Church to prepare us to receive grace and to sanctify our daily life. Blessings are of primary importance. Every baptized person is called to be a blessing, and to bless. Sacraments and sacramentals can sanctify almost every event of our lives with God's grace. In addition, various forms of popular piety nourish the Church.

The Sacrament of Baptism

Baptism is God's most beautiful and magnificent gift....We call it gift, grace, anointing, enlightenment, garment of immortality, bath of rebirth, seal and most precious gift. –Saint Gregory Nazianzen

69. What does Baptism do for us?

Baptism gives us new life in Christ. It is necessary for salvation, as is the Church, which we enter by Baptism.

70. What is the essential rite of Baptism?

The priest or deacon pours water over or immerses the candidate saying, *I baptize you in the name of the Father, and of the Son, and of the Holy Spirit.*

71. What are the effects of Baptism?

In Baptism we are freed of original sin, reborn as adopted children of God, and regenerated in the Holy Spirit. Baptism makes us members of Christ, incorporates us into His Church and makes us sharers in His mission.

Baptism imprints on our souls an indelible spiritual character, which sets us apart for worship. Baptism can therefore never be repeated.

72. How are we changed through Baptism?

In Baptism we die to the world and put on Christ, sharing in the priesthood of all believers. We are all baptized into one body, including those Christians not yet in full communion with the Catholic Church, who are to be accepted as our brethren.

73. Can anyone be saved without Baptism?

Those who die for the faith, catechumens who die before being baptized, and all who, without knowing of the Church, seek under the action of grace for God and strive to serve Him, can be saved without Baptism.

74. What is the normal age for Baptism?

Since her early days, the Church has baptized infants, for Baptism is a grace, an unearned gift from God. The Church invites us to pray for unbaptized children who have died, entrusting them to the mercy of God.

The Sacrament of Confirmation

Then they laid hands on them and they received the holy Spirit.
–Acts 8:17

75. What are the sacraments of Initiation?

Baptism, Confirmation and Eucharist are the sacraments of Christian Initiation. Confirmation completes and *confirms* baptismal grace in the believer, and thus all ought to receive it.

The Sacrament of Confirmation gives the gift of the Holy Spirit, rooting us more firmly in our divine sonship. It fortifies our bond with the Church, strengthens us, and gives us courage to bear witness to Jesus and the gospel in word and deed.

In the Eastern Rite, a priest administers Chrismation immediately after Baptism, followed by the Eucharist. In the Latin Rite the bishop normally administers Confirmation after the age of reason has been reached, signifying the bond of the confirmed to the Body of Christ.

The Sacrament of the Holy Eucharist

I am the living bread that came down from heaven; whoever eats this bread will live forever; and the bread that I will give is my flesh for the life of the world. –John 6:51

76. What is the Eucharist?

The Eucharist (*eucharistein—thanksgiving*) is the heart and summit of the Church's life. In the Eucharist, Jesus gives us His Body and Blood, His very self. Jesus gave us the Eucharist so that He could always be with us, His beloved, in a real and substantial way, and make us sharers in His Passover.

77. How can we respond to the Eucharist?

Jesus gives Himself to us in the Eucharist so that we can give ourselves to Him in love. In Holy Communion we are united with Jesus and with all the members of the Body of Christ, the Church.

78. What does the Mass, the Eucharistic celebration, include?

The Eucharistic celebration includes the proclamation of God's Word, thanksgiving for all God's blessings, especially His Son, consecration of bread and wine into the Body and Blood of Christ, and reception of Holy Communion. Christ's Passion, Death, and Resurrection are made present again as Christ our high priest offers the sacrifice of Himself through the priest.

79. What part of Jesus do we receive in the Eucharist?

In the Eucharist, the bread and wine is changed into the fullness of Christ Jesus Himself, His Body and His Blood, with His Soul and His Divinity.

80. What are the requirements to receive Holy Communion?

The Church encourages frequent Communion, requiring it at least once a year. We must be in the state of grace to receive Communion, which increases our union with the Lord, forgives our venial sins, keeps us from serious sin, and reinforces our unity with the whole Church. We need to fast from all food and drink, except water, for one hour before Communion.

1. What are some of the names of this Sacrament?

There is a deep richness to this wonder of all wonders. Some names are:

The Holy Sacrifice of the Mass

Holy Mass

The Lord's Supper

The Breaking of the Bread

The Holy and Divine Liturgy

The Sacred Mysteries

Holy Communion

The Sacrament of Penance and Reconciliation

And when he had said this, he breathed on them and said to them, Receive the holy Spirit. Whose sins you forgive are forgiven them, and whose sins you retain are retained." –John 20:22-23

As wonderful as Baptism is, we can weaken and even lose God's life within us by sin, which wounds God, our fellow believers, and ourselves. There is no evil graver than sin, which harms so many. Thankfully, Jesus has given His Church the remedy for this universal sickness. In the sacrament of Penance, also called Reconciliation or Confession, God forgives our sins.

2. What does the Sacrament of Reconciliation consist of?

The Church Fathers speak of two conversions: the waters of Baptism and the tears of repentance. Through the Sacrament of Penance, which consists of repentance, confession of sins, and reparation, God, who is rich in mercy, restores us to communion with Himself. Christ, through the priest, absolves us of all sin.

3. What is the difference between perfect and imperfect contrition?

Perfect contrition is repentance arising from a deep love of God; imperfect contrition arises from other motives. We must confess to a priest all the unconfessed grave sins we remember. He then proposes a penance to help us repair the harm caused by sin.

84. What are the effects of the Sacrament of Penance?

In the Sacrament of Penance we are reconciled with God and the Church; the eternal punishment incurred by mortal sins is remitted, as is some or all the temporal punishment of sin. In addition, we regain a serenely peaceful conscience and an increase of spiritual fortitude to help us fight the good fight.

The Anointing of the Sick

Is anyone among you sick? He should summon the presbyters of the church, and they should pray over him and anoint (him) with oil in the name of the Lord, and the prayer of faith will save the sick person, and the Lord will raise him up. If he has committed any sins, he will be forgiven. —James 5:14-15

Humanity has long struggled with illness and suffering. Affliction can lead either to bitterness and despair or to a child-like trust in God, who is with us and has come to heal us. Jesus healed all who were brought to Him and gave His disciples healing power as well. Through the ages the Holy Spirit has poured out the charism of healing to manifest the grace of the risen Lord.

85. How does the Anointing of the Sick work?

The sacrament of the Anointing of the Sick confers a special grace of healing on the believer experiencing serious illness or old age. A priest administers this sacrament by anointing with blessed oil the forehead and hands of the sick person, laying on his hands and praying for God's healing grace.

86. What are the effects of the Anointing of the Sick?

The Anointing of the Sick unites the sick to the Passion of Christ, for their good and that of the whole Church. It imparts strength, peace, and courage; it forgives sins, restores health if it is conducive to salvation, and prepares for their passing over into eternal life. In this final Passover Mother Church accompanies her children, to surrender them into the hands of their Compassionate Father, looking forward to their final Resurrection and eternal joy. And that's good news!

The Sacrament of Holy Orders

For this reason, I remind you to stir into flame the gift of God that you have through the imposition of my hands. –2 Timothy 1:6

Jesus chose apostles to follow Him, continue His ministry, and shepherd His flock. Through the Sacrament of Holy Orders, the Church ordains bishops, priests, and deacons to serve the People of God, continuing the mission entrusted to the apostles. Ordination imprints upon the souls of these men an indelible spiritual mark, or character, a seal that can never be removed.

87. How are bishops the successors of the apostles today?

As successor of the apostles, a bishop receives the fullness of Holy Orders, integrating him into the college of bishops and making him the visible head of his particular church (diocese). He shares in apostolic responsibility and mission as true pastor and teacher under the Pope, Bishop of Rome.

88. What is the ministry of priests?

As co-workers of the bishop, priests preach the Gospel, shepherd the faithful, and celebrate divine worship.

89. What is the ministry of deacons?

As servants, deacons are ordained to serve in the ministry of the Word, divine worship, pastoral government and the service of charity. Since Vatican II, married men can receive the permanent Diaconate, thus greatly enriching the Body of Christ.

90. How is a priest ordained?

In the sacrament of Holy Orders, the bishop imposes his hands on the candidate, consecrating him to the Lord and entreating the Holy Spirit for the graces needed for his ministry. The Church ordains only baptized men who, called to the presbyterate, are ready to embrace celibacy. Holy Orders marks the ordained with an indelible spiritual imprint, or seal, which configures them to Christ.

The Sacrament of Matrimony

That is why a man leaves his father and mother and clings to his wife, and the two of them become one body. —Genesis 2:24

In the Marriage covenant a man and a woman enter into an intimate communion of life and love ordered to their good and to the generation and education of children. Jesus raised marriage to a sacramental dignity at the wedding in Cana. Marriage is for the companionship and mutual love of the spouses and for the procreation of children.

91. What are the effects of the sacrament of Matrimony?

The sacrament of matrimony symbolizes the faithful love of Christ for His Bride, the Church. It perfects the love of husband and wife, strengthens their unity, consecrates them, and makes them holy as they journey together to the Father's house.

92. What did Jesus say about marriage?

Some Pharisees approached him, and tested him, saying, "Is it lawful for a man to divorce his wife for any cause whatever?" He said in reply, "Have you not read that from the beginning the Creator 'made them male and female' and said, 'For this reason a man shall leave his father and mother and be joined to his wife, and the two shall become one flesh'? So they are no longer two, but one flesh. Therefore, what God has joined together, no human being must separate."
—Matthew 19:3-6

93. How does the Sacrament of Matrimony help a married couple?

God established marriage to be a blessing and a deep joy. Unfortunately, discord, infidelity, and conflicts can threaten marital unity, stability, and openness to children. Without Christ Jesus, man and woman cannot achieve their God-ordained union. Thankfully, the Holy Spirit and the sacraments are ever available to help married couples renew and strengthen their love.

94. What is necessary for a sacramental Christian Marriage?

There are three elements necessary for a sacramental marriage:

Both partners must give their free consent

Both must affirm their choice of a life-long, exclusive union.

Both must be open to children.

95. What are the effects of the Sacrament of Matrimony?

A Perpetual and Exclusive Bond

A valid marriage brings about a perpetual and exclusive bond between the spouses. In Christian marriage, the spouses are strengthened and consecrated by a special sacrament.

Never to be Broken

The mutual consent of a married couple is sealed by God Himself and results in an institution which is confirmed by divine law and accepted in the eyes of society.

A marriage bond which is concluded and consummated by baptized spouses can never be dissolved. The spouses' consent and consummation forge an irrevocable covenant which even the Church cannot break.

Christ's Graces

Because of their Christian state, spouses receive graces to complete their love, to help them obtain holiness and to welcome and educate their children.

Jesus encounters the spouses through the Sacrament of Matrimony. He gives them the strength to begin again when they fail, to forgive each other, to be subject to one another and to enjoy a taste of the heavenly wedding feast.

How can I even express the happiness of a marriage joined by the Church? How wonderful the bond between two believers. Where the flesh is one, one also is the spirit.

–Tertullian

DEAR PARENTS OF A CONFIRMATION CANDIDATE,

Congratulations! Your child has chosen to prepare for the Sacrament of Confirmation. Like all sacraments, Confirmation is not a reward, but a gift, a gift of mercy and deeper life from God our Father.

You've already been journeying on the road of life with your son or daughter for a good bit of time! Now is a great opportunity to stop and reflect on where you've been, where you are, and where you're going on your faith journey, both alone and with your child.

This section is a resource, a guide of sorts to help you hopefully gain some new insights and understandings about your teenager and your relationship with him or her.

YOUR ROLE

As parents, you are the primary educators of your children in the faith. The word "educate" comes from the Latin *educare:* "to lead out of." Your mission is to help lead your child from the darkness of ignorance into the light of faith. From the beginning, even in the womb, a child senses his mother's feelings. Once born, a child is more affected than we may realize by Dad and Mom, on all fronts. That means you *matter* to your child, perhaps more than you are aware. You are at the very heart of his or her understanding of God, Jesus, the Holy Spirit, and the experiences of our faith.

Your parish church or school is there to support you, but you are called to help complete the Baptismal life you brought to your children. So we should perhaps begin by asking, "How is *your* soul?"

As with all things in our busy lives, we can tend to allow our spiritual life go on auto-pilot, or maybe regress to a check list: Sunday Mass? *Check.* Grace at meals? *Yes and no.* Morning/Night prayer: *Sometimes,* etc. But God wants more than a check list. He wants you to allow Him to love, heal, strengthen, and guide you every day. He wants to flood your soul with His love, and to bring you to a depth of fulfillment you may have never dreamed possible. As Saint Augustine wrote, "God loves each of us as if there were only one of us."

So, the best way to encourage your teen to deepen their faith life is to first deepen your own. The Spirit of God in you will affect your child, perhaps when and where you least expect.

Take a moment and read the words of the prayer that the bishop or his delegate will pray over your son or daughter at their Confirmation:

> "All-powerful God, Father of our Lord Jesus Christ, by water and the Holy Spirit you freed your sons and daughters from sin and gave them new life. Send your Holy Spirit upon them to be their helper and guide. Give them the spirit of wisdom and understanding, the spirit of right judgment and courage, the spirit of knowledge and reverence. Fill them with the spirit of wonder and awe in your presence."
>
> *–The Rite of Confirmation*

HELPING YOUR SON OR DAUGHTER GROW IN FAITH

How can you help your child become more aware of the movement of the Holy Spirit in their hearts and lives?

Here are some suggestions:

- Talk to them about their faith, their relationship with Jesus, and with the Church. Do not be put off even if they answer you with a blank stare.

- Ask them why they want to be confirmed. What does it mean to them?

- Talk about the sacraments, especially Eucharist and Reconciliation. Do they feel nourished through them?

- What does your child think it means for them to be Catholic? Do they see themselves as a child of God? What does it mean to be a saint?

It's very normal to feel somewhat awkward or inadequate striking out on this conversation, but try not to let those feelings keep you from sharing. It's good to show your teen they can feel comfortable talking with you about the joys and struggles of faith that we all experience.

Your child is unique, with his or her own personality, gifts, and talents. It is good to affirm your children, to let them know what you see in them. Ask the Holy Spirit to help you see your child's gifts and potential, and to share those with him or her. This helps a teen discover their vocation, what God is calling them to do with their life.

It is also good to pray with your child and to encourage them to pray about their mission in life. They can do this though prayers and novenas, especially asking the intercession of their Confirmation saint.

All of this preparation will help your son or daughter to experience more fully the presence of the Holy Spirit. There are a number of great resources available, including *YouCat (Youth Catechism of the Catholic Church)* and many others.

Your role as parent of a Confirmation candidate, then, is to first of all start or continue to actively seek the Lord through your own faith life. This is an extension of the commitment you undertook at your child's Baptism. In Confirmation, your role is more of a spiritual companion and advisor, as your child and you now have a golden opportunity to grow in your understanding of your faith and traditions. If possible, attend whatever catechetical sessions your church may provide for your own faith formation. Remember, you're not alone! With the help of the parish, you will be better suited to share your faith journey and help your child in their own decision to grow in their faith.

But seek first the kingdom (of God) and his
righteousness, and all these things
will be given you besides.
–Matthew 6:33

GUIDING YOUR ADOLESCENT

God designed adolescence, so we as parents can relax a bit when the changes it brings—puberty, new ways of thinking, a wider sphere of social relationships and activities, and greater autonomy—present the family with a whole new range of challenges.

Do any of these challenges that parents face with their teens (and their teen with them) look familiar? What would you add?

Teen Independence

Parental Flexibility

Permeable Boundaries

Parental Authority

Influence of Friends

Fluctuating Independence and Dependence

Relationships with Extended Family

HEALTHY AND HOLY

Confirmation can be a time for you to identify what you as a parent can do to help build your child into a healthy adult. Pope Benedict said that God only wants to give us "life and love." Developing certain life skills can help your son or daughter achieve wholeness and holiness.

It is possible to build up your child directly and indirectly. You as parents, and to some extent, their teachers, friends, and others, can encourage and boost your son or daughter directly by:

- Comforting your child when he or she feels hurt by another's unkind action or word.

- Listening to your child when they feel like talking, regardless of the time or place.

- Accepting them as they are: their clothing, hair style, etc.

- Cheering them on as their biggest fan during their sports events, extracurricular activities, and whatever interests they engage in.

- Encouraging them in their hard times.

Other ways to build up your child directly:

- Tell your son or daughter how much you love them.

- Hug them. They, and you, may feel uncomfortable at first, but keep it up and it will become a way to show your affection more fully.

- Be consistent with your rules.

- Encourage self-discovery.

- Create a family motto.

- Allow your child their own space, but let them know you are available.

- Ask your child, "What one new thing did you learn today?"

You can build up your child indirectly through your commitments, attitudes, values, and skills. These can all support a person from within, and are often shared through modeling. Have you ever:

- Modeled lifelong learning by taking a class or doing special reading on a topic?

- Volunteered to serve others as an individual or with your family?

- Spent time visiting with your child's friends?

Other ways to build up your son or daughter indirectly:

- Share your own dreams and goals with them.

- Serve as a family. Gather together and feed the homeless, collect baby clothes for Crisis pregnancy centers, donate blood. There are many ways to "love one another" as Jesus has loved us.

- Stop using negative humor, uncalled-for teasing, "put downs," etc.

- Encourage your son or daughter to dream big, and to set meaningful goals as a way to progress toward their dreams.

- Continue to grow in your own faith through reading, discussion or participation in faith sharing groups.

HELPING YOUR CHILD CHOOSE A SPONSOR

The primary responsibility of the Confirmation Sponsor is to provide the candidate prayerful support and guidance in his or her Christian walk and to "take care that the confirmed person behaves as a true witness of Christ and faithfully fulfills the obligations inherent in this sacrament" *(Code of Canon Law 892).*

In a word, a sponsor is the special person chosen by your child to represent the faith community at the Rite of Confirmation. A sponsor walks with the candidate for Confirmation, supporting and nurturing their faith.

Because Confirmation completes Baptism, the Church encourages that one of the child's godparents be their sponsor as well. A sponsor should be a mature person of faith who is highly convinced that their faith makes a difference.

POPE FRANCIS ON THE GIFT OF THE HOLY SPIRIT

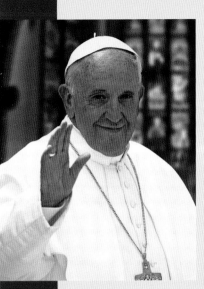

"We can do nothing without the strength of the Holy Spirit: it is the Spirit that gives us the strength to go forward. ... What is Jesus' identity card in the synagogue of Nazareth? ... 'The Spirit of the Lord is upon me, because He has anointed me to preach good news to the poor' (Luke 4:18). Jesus presents himself in the synagogue of his village as the Anointed, He who was anointed by the Spirit. Jesus is full of the Holy Spirit and is the source of the Spirit promised by the Father. The Spirit is in our heart, in our soul. And the Spirit guides us in life so that we become right salt and right light for men. ... I wonder: how is it seen that we have received the Gift of the Spirit? It is seen if we carry out the works of the Spirit, if we pronounce words taught by the Spirit.

"The Spirit frees hearts chained by fear. To those content with half measures he inspires whole-hearted generosity. He opens hearts that are closed. He impels the comfortable to go out and serve. He drives the self-satisfied to set out in new directions. He makes the lukewarm thrill to new dreams. That is what it means to change hearts.

"May each of us grow in gratitude for the gift received at our Confirmation and open our hearts ever more fully to the creativity of the Spirit who makes all things new."

THE MAGNIFICAT

And Mary said:
"My soul proclaims the greatness of the Lord;
my spirit rejoices in God my savior.
For he has looked upon his handmaid's lowliness;
behold, from now on will all ages call me blessed.
The Mighty One has done great things for me,
and holy is his name.
His mercy is from age to age
to those who fear him.
He has shown might with his arm,
dispersed the arrogant of mind and heart.
He has thrown down the rulers from their thrones
but lifted up the lowly.
The hungry he has filled with good things;
the rich he has sent away empty.
He has helped Israel his servant,
remembering his mercy,
according to his promise to our fathers,
to Abraham and to his descendants forever."

–Luke 1:46-55